The Lord Is My Shepherd

HAROLD S. KUSHNER

The Lord
Is My Shepherd

HEALING WISDOM
OF THE TWENTY-THIRD PSALM

Alfred A. Knopf New York 2003

THIS IS A BORZOI BOOK
PUBLISHED BY ALFRED A. KNOPF

Library of Congress Cataloging-in-Publication Data

Kushner, Harold S.
The Lord is my shepherd : healing wisdom of the Twenty-third
Psalm / Harold S. Kushner.—1st ed.
p. cm.
ISBN 1-4000-4056-6 (alk. paper)
1. Bible O.T. Psalms XXIII—Criticism, interpretation, etc.
I. Title.

BS145023rd .K87 2003   223'.206—dc21   2002043441

Manufactured in the United States of America
First Edition

For Suzette
For she has been with me
Through so many peaks and valleys.

A psalm of David:

The Lord is my shepherd; I shall not want.

He makes me to lie down in green pastures,

He leads me beside the still waters.

He restores my soul.

He guides me in straight paths for His Name's sake.

*Yea, though I walk through the valley of the shadow
 of death,*

I will fear no evil

For Thou art with me.

Thy rod and Thy staff, they comfort me.

*Thou preparest a table before me in the presence of
 mine enemies.*

Thou anointest my head with oil,

My cup runneth over.

*Surely goodness and mercy shall follow me all the
 days of my life,*

And I shall dwell in the House of the Lord forever.

Contents

Contents

The Lord Is My Shepherd

First Words

I have been thinking about the ideas in this book for more than forty years, since I was first ordained as a rabbi. Every time I would read the Twenty-third Psalm at a funeral or memorial service, or at the bedside of an ailing congregant, I would be struck by its power to comfort the grieving and calm the fearful. But the real impetus for this book came in the wake of the terrible events of September 11, 2001. In the days following the attacks, people on the street and television interviewers would ask me, "Where was God? How could God let this happen?" I found myself responding, "God's promise was never that life would be fair. God's promise was that, when we had to confront the unfairness of life, we would not have to do it alone for He would be with us." And I realized I had found that answer in the Twenty-third Psalm.

I have been fortunate, in writing this book, to benefit from the guidance of two very capable editors. This is my sixth book written with the help of James H. Silberman. His is a distinguished name in the publishing industry, and he has been an unfailing source of encouragement and direction. It is my second book shared with Jonathan Segal of Alfred A. Knopf. Jonathan is a marvelously skilled editor whose suggestions helped give the book the focus and direction it needed. I am grateful to both of them.

My longtime agent, Peter Ginsberg, played a key role as matchmaker for this book, and I thank him for it.

But mostly I am grateful to Suzette, my wife of forty-three years, for her patience and encouragement through all the months it took me to bring forth this book. I could not have done it without her.

CHAPTER ONE

A Psalm of David

C an fifteen beautiful lines from a single page of the Bible change your life? I believe they can, if you are willing to open your heart to their magic. Listen closely to them, read them with an open mind and an open heart, and you will find the answers to questions you are asking, questions about yourself, the people around you, and the world in which you and they live.

I would guess that there is one, and only one, chapter of the Bible that most people in the English-speaking world know by heart. We may remember a lot of stories about Adam and Eve, Noah, Joseph, and Moses. We may be able to recite the Ten Commandments, parts of the Sermon on the Mount, and other passages that have entered into our literature. But when it comes to an entire chapter, I suspect that the only one we remember completely is chapter twenty-three of the Book of Psalms, the

Twenty-third Psalm, "The Lord is my shepherd, I shall not want. . . ."

Even if you cannot recite the entire psalm perfectly, you know it well enough to say it along with a congregation, the way many of us sing along with "The Star-Spangled Banner" at a baseball game. We are so familiar with the Twenty-third Psalm that when a new translation of the Bible comes along, using archaeological and linguistic evidence to help us understand more accurately what the original Hebrew and Greek meant to say, we are uncomfortable with the "improvements." We welcome the rewording of the stories, stripped of the Elizabethan vocabulary of the four-hundred-year-old King James translation (done in the time of Shakespeare). We don't miss the use of "begat" and "wouldst" and "thee" and "thou." But when it comes to our favorite psalm, we crave familiarity more than accuracy.

Why do we love this psalm so much, more than any of the other 149 psalms in the Bible? Why do we reach for it at moments of personal distress, cherishing its recitation at funerals and memorial services? It is a beautiful literary creation, but the anthologies are full of beautiful writings, and they don't capture our hearts as the Twenty-third Psalm does. In just a few lines, it conveys the distilled wisdom of generations, offering us a way of seeing the world that renders it less frightening, teaching us to deal with the loss of people we love and with conflict with people who don't like us or who treat us badly. It shows us how to recognize the presence of God at times and in places where we might think God was absent or when we might be so distracted by our own concerns that we would overlook God's presence. It has the power to teach us to think differently and, as a result, to act differently.

Science, Albert Einstein once said, can tell us a lot about the universe—how old it is, how vast it is, what laws of physics control it. But he went on to say that science is powerless to answer the most important question of all: Is the universe a friendly place, supportive of human hopes and aspirations?

The Twenty-third Psalm, with its image of the Lord as our shepherd, responds to that concern. It gives us an answer, not in theological language but in beautifully crafted words and skillfully chosen images, and we respond to its honesty and optimism as much as to the beauty of its language. It comforts us with its familiar words and images, but its message goes well beyond comfort. It does not simply offer us the prospect of a better, safer world beyond this one. It teaches us to look at the world we live in clearly and without illusions, but at the same time to see it as a world in which we can live courageously, doing good for ourselves and others. Our world may not be a perfect world, but it is God's world, and that makes all the difference. Yes, the world may be dangerous, it admits, but God is there to take care of us, to help us, even as a shepherd cares for his sheep in a world of dangerous predators and threats of accident. The world may be a frightening place, but it becomes less frightening when we know that God is here with us. As one writer has put it, sometimes God calms the storm, but sometimes God lets the storm rage and calms the frightened child.

The psalm does not deny the shattering reality of death and loss, nor does it minimize how painful death and loss can be to us. It never asks us to pretend, as some religious teachings do, that death does not change things, that moving from life to death is no different than moving from New York to Chicago. It acknowledges the emotional darkness we find ourselves in when a loved one is dying or has died, the "valley of the shadow of death." But instead of cursing a God who permits our loved ones to die, it introduces us to a God who is with us in our pain, and who leads us through the dark valley back into the light. It summons us to live bravely, to go forward with our lives in the confidence that we are not alone.

The psalm does not offer us the pious hope that, if we are good people, life will be easy, as some religious texts do. The author of the psalm has enemies. He has known failure. He has lost people he loved. In the process, he has learned that life is not easy. Life is a challenge, and he has grown stronger as, with God's help, he met the challenges of life. He is a better person, a wiser, stronger person than he would have been, had life not challenged him to grow.

The psalm can teach us another valuable lesson as well: Much of the time, we cannot control what happens to us. But we can always control how we respond to what happens to us. If we cannot choose to be lucky, to be talented, to be loved, we can choose to be grateful, to be content with who we are and what we have, and to act accordingly.

In a mere fifty-seven words of Hebrew and just about twice that number in English translation, the author of the Twenty-third Psalm gives us an entire theology, a more practical theology than we can find in many books. He teaches us to look at the world and see it as God would have us see it. If we are anxious, the psalm gives us courage and we overcome our fears. If we are grieving, it offers comfort and we find our way through the valley of the shadow. If our lives are embittered by unpleasant people, it teaches us how to deal with them. If the world threatens to wear us down, the psalm guides us to replenish our souls. If we are obsessed with what we lack, it teaches us gratitude for what we have. And most of all, if we feel alone and adrift in a friendless world, it offers us the priceless reassurance that "Thou art with me."

Who wrote the Twenty-third Psalm, this compact spiritual masterpiece that we love so much? Alas, that is a question we will never be able to answer. People of the ancient world had a different understanding of what it meant to "write" a literary or liturgical work. They understood that, just as "it takes a village to raise a child," it takes an entire culture to write a psalm. How could one person take credit for a literary creation and deny credit to his parents who raised him, his teachers who educated him, his religious leaders who inspired him, and most of all God who was the ultimate source of his inspiration? I cannot imagine Homer getting up in ancient Greece and saying, Here is a poem I wrote about the Trojan war. He is much more likely to have said, This is the story of the fall of Troy, playing down his personal role in putting it into words.

Many people hold to the tradition that King David wrote all 150 of the psalms, and indeed the Twenty-third Psalm begins, as so many do, with the words "A Psalm of David." Many years ago, I wrote my doctoral dissertation on the history of the Book of Psalms and found myself concurring with the virtually unanimous opinion of Bible scholars that King David could not have written all of the psalms. Some of them refer to historical events that happened hundreds of years after his death, such as the Babylonian Exile. Some employ Hebrew words and grammatical forms that were not in use until long after David's time.

It may be that King David composed a few psalms (the prophet Amos, who lived only a few hundred years after the time of David, refers to him as a musician and composer). If he did, the Twenty-third Psalm may have been one of them, featuring imagery that would have come naturally to this shepherd-warrior-king. It may also be that "a psalm of David" means "a psalm in the style of David" or "a psalm composed in honor of King David" or in honor of a later king, a descendant of the House of David.

But although we can never know the name of the man who wrote this masterpiece of faith and comfort, this masterful guide to how we might think and act, we learn a lot about him by reading his words. We can see the psalm as the story of a journey, one that began with his living a pleasant, comfortable life, symbolized by lush, soft grass and cool water. Then something happened to shatter that comfortable life. It may have been a life-threatening illness. It may have been betrayal or rejection by people around him. But most likely it was the death of someone about whom he cared deeply. He found himself in despair, his world grown dark. Images of gloom, of darkness, dominated his thoughts. It seemed that there was no point to his going on with his life. In his despair, he cried out to God, and a miracle happened. The miracle was not that the dead came back to life, or that the man's health and wealth were restored. The miracle was that he found life worth living. God answered his prayer not by replacing what he had lost, but by taking him by the hand and guiding him through the "valley of the shadow of death." To his amazement, he who no longer believed that the sun was shining anywhere found himself standing in the sunshine again. The past had not changed, but the future suddenly seemed more inviting. I can imagine the author writing this psalm to share with everyone who would hear it or read it what he had just learned about God and life.

I have been drawn to the Twenty-third Psalm throughout my adult life, as a student of the Bible, as a pastor, as a husband, as a father, and as a child of aging parents. I have marveled at its almost magical ability to soothe and comfort people in pain. I have found that, the closer I look, the more the psalm has to say to me. I would like to share with you the insights born of a lifetime of studying these familiar words, examining them line by line in the hope that they will enrich your life as they have enriched mine.

One grammatical note on reading the psalm in translation: In the Hebrew Bible, God is grammatically masculine, but functionally God is both masculine and feminine. That is, the psalm refers to God as "He," as does the Bible as a whole. But the psalm, and the Bible, will often show that same God in a feminine dimension, acting more like a mother than a father. Accordingly, I will refer to God as "He," both when I am quoting the psalm and when I am discussing it, not because I believe that God is a male but because the English language offers me no suitable alternative. I am not prepared to reduce God to an "It."

In the end, there is no explaining why we love a certain

piece of literature any more than we can explain why we love a certain person. But perhaps we will come to understand this most beloved of all the psalms, and in the process understand ourselves and our world a little better, and learn to live in that world with faith and courage. It is a psalm that has the power to change a person's life.

CHAPTER TWO

The Lord Is My Shepherd

The earliest ancestors of the Hebrew people who gave us the Bible were nomads, owning no property, bound to no one location but traveling with their flocks and herds wherever there was pastureland for the animals to graze on. Sometimes this involved a journey of a few miles, sometimes it meant longer trips from drought-plagued areas to well-watered neighboring countries. Generations later, their descendants would become farmers and learn to see life as a partnership between the hard work of the farmer and the grace of heaven sending the rain in its season. Later still, some of them would be artisans and merchants. Their understanding of religion would expand to include the ethics of honoring contracts and treating workers and customers fairly. But they never forgot their origins, telling stories of Abraham, Moses, and David tending their sheep. Long after they stopped being shepherds themselves, they retained the mind-set of the shepherd guarding his flock with love for every tender lamb, dedicated to protecting them from the world's dangers. And in their poetry, they pictured God as a shepherd.

To say "the Lord is my shepherd" is to say that we live in an unpredictable, often terrifying world, ever mindful of all the bad things that might happen to us and to those around us. The philosopher William James writes of "the pit of insecurity beneath the surface of life." But despite it all, we can get up every morning to face that world because we know that there is Someone in that world who cares about us and tries to keep us safe. To philosophers and theologians, God may be the First Cause, the Unmoved Mover. But to people like us, what is most important about God is that He is the Presence that makes the world seem less frightening.

The primary message of the Twenty-third Psalm is not that bad things will never happen to us. It is that we will not have to face those bad things alone, "for Thou art with me." The newspaper headlines will still speak of violence and tragedy. The news bulletins on radio and television will be no less alarming. But we will be able to face the world with more courage and more confidence because we will not be facing it alone.

I have spent my adult life teaching people that religion is first and foremost a source of community (the word "religion" comes from a Latin root meaning "to bind together" as in the word "ligament"; religion binds people together to deal with life's joyous and sorrowful moments) and that faith in God is first and foremost an issue of morality, that there is only one God and that He demands righteous behavior, proclaiming that certain things are wrong, not just illegal or unpleasant but wrong. But my congregants over the years have taught me that I was offering them a graduate course in theology while they were still operating at an introductory level, understanding religion and faith in God in terms of personal security. Their souls craved a God who would make them feel safe. Desperately aware of our vulnerability, all too often reminded of our powerlessness when it comes to the things that matter most to us—life, health, being loved, the well-being of our families—we crave the reassurance that the guiding spirit of the universe knows us and cares about us. As the Reverend Forrest Church has written, "Religion is our human response to the dual reality of being alive and knowing that we have to die."

Psychologists tell us that young children have a "morality of security." "Good" is anything that makes them feel safe; "bad" is anything that makes them feel anxious. God and parents are important in children's lives because they help children feel secure in an insecure world. I have seen a book for young children published by an Orthodox Jewish group that tells children that if they pray to God to keep them safe, they will be able to cross streets without being hit by a car. (My reaction: You can believe it if you want to, but don't try it. You're likely to end up in the hospital with as many physical problems as theological ones.)

There is a part of us that never entirely outgrows that kind of thinking. Just as many children are in the habit of saying a prayer at bedtime to help them feel safe in the knowledge that God is watching over them, there is a prayer adults recite in the Jewish evening service that asks God to watch over us as we lie down to sleep, keeping us safe from harm and misfortune. I often think of it as the spiritual equivalent of a night-light, letting us close our eyes without worrying about the dangers that might lurk in the darkness. Worrying about them is God's job.

When we are young, our parents play that role. They represent security, the promise to keep us safe. We may resent the pleasures they deny us and the restrictions they impose on us ("don't play in the street"; "no snacks before dinner"). But at some level, we instinctively know that they are doing that out of love, for our own good. Children who are constantly testing the limits of their parents' rules are gratified to win some arguments but would likely panic if their parents never said no to them, like a person who feels the wall move when he leans against it.

As we grow older, we discover that our parents can't always keep us safe. Favorite toys break and can't be mended. We get sick, we fall down and hurt ourselves, and our parents replace the promise of safety with the offer of the reassurance of caring and love. They dote on us, dry our tears, bring us medicine and chicken soup, constantly ask how we are feeling. Should we be sick or injured because we ignored their advice, spurned the sweater in cold weather, drove carelessly, we experience the reassuring miracle of forgiveness. We learn that parental love is absolute, not conditional. We don't have to earn it with good grades, achievements, or even obedience. We deserve it for being who we are, and for their being who they are.

When we grow into adolescence, nature compels us to declare our independence from our families of origin, but we never outgrow the yearning for someone who will make us feel safe and cared for in an unsafe world and special in a crowded, impersonal world. George Gershwin captured that sense of longing when he composed the romantic ballad "Someone to Watch Over Me." As adolescents and young adults, we reach out to boyfriends and girlfriends not only because of surging hormones but also out of a need to feel cherished. Some psychologists speculate that we end up marrying people who, at a subconscious level, remind us of our fathers and mothers, not out of some unresolved Oedipal complex but out of a quest to recapture the sense of being loved and protected that we knew as children.

I remember a woman from my congregation, a pillar of the synagogue, who came to see me one day, distraught because her son was marrying a young woman of a different faith. "She's a lovely girl and I don't begrudge him his happiness," she said to me. "They've even agreed to raise their children as Jews. What hurts so much is that I feel his choice of a wife is a way of rejecting me and everything I've tried to teach him." I met the young couple to hear their side of the story, and within minutes I was struck by how much the young woman resembled her fiancé's mother. She looked like a younger version of her future mother-in-law (no wonder the mother liked her). She had the same high energy level and many of the same interests. She even bossed her fiancé around much as his mother did. I began to suspect that this young man was saying to himself, "I've finally broken free of my controlling mother. I'm going to marry a woman my mother finds unacceptable and there's nothing she can do about it," when, in fact, he was working to replicate the home and the family in which he had grown up.

Women may be attracted to men who are good-looking or good dancers, but they will find themselves drawn, without immediately understanding why, to men who they sense will protect them and their future children physically, financially, and emotionally. Men may say they are looking for an attractive woman who will also be a good mother to their children, but they will find something powerfully attractive about a woman who will praise them and make them feel like winners just as their mothers did. In William Goldman's novel *The Color of Light,* the narrator, as a college freshman, sees the stunningly beautiful girl of his dreams marry an older, better looking, more dashing man. Years later, the narrator runs into her again and learns that her husband has left her for a plain, unattractive woman. The attractive, rejected ex-wife cannot understand why. The reader might well suspect that the husband felt threatened by her beauty and her independence, and chose to leave her before she could leave him. Or it may be that, at age twenty-five, winning the heart of the most desirable girl on campus made that man feel special. He felt like a winner. But after ten years of marriage, his own insecurities made him search for a different kind of specialness with a very different woman. It could well have been that his wife no longer praised and admired him on a daily basis, as she had done when they first met, and that he wanted a woman who would.

I shared that theory, that we seek to marry someone who makes us feel special the way our parents did, with a friend, who responded, "But what about those of us who were never made to feel that way by our parents when we were young? Who are we attracted to?" I thought about that for a moment and suggested that some of those people end up marrying spouses who will mistreat them just as their parents did, whether because it is the only kind of relationship they have known or because they have grown up believing that they deserve it. Others will look for what they could not get from parents in the person they marry, maybe marrying at a young age someone who would be part parent and part spouse. Some will devote their lives to a cause or a leader, a religious or philosophical guru who will promise to be the all-wise, all-loving father they never had. And many of us, disappointed in our parents in big or small ways, will turn to God, the superparent who, more than any earthly parent, teacher, or political leader, has the power to protect us and the compassion to put up with us, no matter who we are or what we do.

A skeptic might ask, If the Lord is my shepherd, if it's His responsibility to keep me safe, why isn't He doing a better job of it? Why is it that I can never watch the news on television or open my morning paper without hearing or reading about some tragedy or crime? Why am I constantly seeing good people dying, good people crippled by illness, good people divorced, fired, cheated? Where is God's saving grace and compassion in all those cases?

We may be able to find the beginning of an answer in what we can think of as the Shepherd's Creed, articulated by Jacob in the Bible when he summarizes his twenty years of working as a shepherd for his father-in-law, Laban. To justify his record of honorable service, Jacob tells Laban (in Genesis 31:38–40), "These twenty years I spent in your service, your ewes and she-goats never miscarried, nor did I feast on rams from your flock. That which was torn by beasts I never brought to you. I myself made good the loss, whether snatched by day or snatched by night.

Heat afflicted me by day and cold by night; sleep fled from my eyes." Scholars explain those two next-to-last verses as referring to the shepherd's right to bring to the owner of the flock the remains of a sheep eaten by wolves or other wild animals, as proof that he had not killed and feasted on it himself and blamed it on a wolf. The shepherd was expected to do his best to fend off predators during the day, but could not reasonably be asked to do so at night, when he was entitled to his sleep and when predators were harder to see.

If that is a portrait of the faithful shepherd, what might the image of the Lord as our shepherd say to those of us who challenge Him by pointing to life's unfairness?

God might say first of all that while He cannot protect every one of us from every misfortune that might befall us, His providence extends to the human race as a whole. Our bodies are fashioned so that, most of the time, they fight off disease and heal from injuries. The tragic stories that grab our attention in the news each day are newsworthy precisely because they are rare. Earthquakes and shark attacks are spectacular but extremely infrequent. Crimes of violence are profoundly upsetting to the victims, but most people will never be victims and most victims will escape with only a financial loss and a bad scare. When terrorists attacked the World Trade Center and the Pentagon on September 11, 2001, we learned something about the psychology of terror: strike one person and frighten ten thousand. The statistical probability of being a victim of terrorism is slight, even if you live in Israel or Colombia. But the victims of terror are chosen so randomly that, despite the statistics, we are all made to feel vulnerable. This is the greatest crime of the terrorist: He not only kills his immediate victims, he robs us all of our sense of security. Clearly, we would all prefer to live in a world where earthquakes and robberies are unknown, but that happens not to be the world in which we live. All we can do is see those things in perspective and not be misled by lurid headlines.

People die, despite the prayers of those who love them. And while we might agree that it would be no blessing to live forever, we might wish to live longer and in better health. God's explanation might be that He has shown us how to minimize the bad things that happen to His creatures. He has blessed us with minds to seek out cures for disease. He has given us memory that we might learn the lessons of the past. Like a good shepherd, He asks that we follow His ways not for His sake but for our own.

One of the lessons I learned from the story of Adam and Eve in the Garden of Eden is that our first ancestors chose to be human rather than to live forever. They chose a sense of morality, a "knowledge of good and evil," rather than immortality. They spurned the Tree of Life, which would have given them eternal life, in favor of the Tree of the Knowledge of Good and Evil, which gave them a conscience. As compensation, God gave humans, who now shared with Him the ability to know good from evil, the gift of His own divine power to create new life. We cheat death, not by living forever, but by bearing, raising, and educating children to keep our souls, our values, and even our names alive. One generation, scarred and often embittered by experience, gives way to another, born in innocence and hope. Like the good shepherd He is, God shows His love for us by enabling us to create new life.

And finally God can assure us that He cares about each one of us, as a shepherd cares for each of his flock. While He cannot keep every one of us safe, He grieves for each of us in our afflictions.

The biblical Book of Numbers, the fourth book of the Hebrew Bible, takes its name from a census of the wandering Israelites, a listing of the population of each tribe and of each clan within each tribe, adding up to a total of slightly more than six hundred thousand souls. Scholars consider the numbers unreliable, and most readers will be tempted to skip that page. But commentators of old operated on the principle that if a page of Scripture seemed lacking in significance, the defect was more likely to be in the reader than in the Bible. Confronting the census tables, they compared God to a shepherd whose flock had been attacked by wolves, even as the Israelites had been attacked by brigands during their wandering. Rather than accept the notion that there were a lot of people before and there were about as many now, God lovingly counts every last one of His flock and grieves for each one that is missing.

One of the greatest artistic creations ever fashioned by human hands is the *Pietà* of Michelangelo, a sculpture done in 1498 when the artist was only twenty-three. It shows Mary the mother of Jesus holding the broken body of her son on her lap, looking at him with such tenderness and sorrow that one does not have to share Christian belief in the theological significance of the Crucifixion to be moved by it. The combination of love and sorrow on Mary's face, the sense of her longing to take onto herself some of her son's pain that she might lessen it, speaks to anyone who has loved another person. There is no questioning its status as a masterpiece of artistic skill. There is only one problem with it: The scene it portrays probably never happened. If you reread the accounts of the Crucifixion in the four gospels, you will find that only in the Gospel of John is Mary even present at the Crucifixion, and even then she is sent away before Jesus dies. In the other three versions, Mary is not listed among the Galilean women witnessing Jesus' death. All accounts of Jesus being taken down from the cross and buried mention other people being involved, but not his mother.

How can Michelangelo's *Pietà* move us so deeply, how can it strike us as so right and so true, if it portrays an event that never took place? Let me suggest that the woman in the sculpture, the figure holding the broken body of the crucified Jesus, looking at it so sadly and tenderly, is not Mary but God, God in His feminine aspect, not the God who created the world and taught us how to live in it, but the God who created life in all of its fragile vulnerability, the way a mother creates life, a God who grieves for His children when they suffer, who suffers with them when they are cruel to one another, when they hurt and kill one another. Every mother, every parent who suffers the loss of a child is reenacting God's grief at the death of any one of His children. As one of America's most prominent clergymen, the Reverend William Sloane Coffin, insisted, reaffirming his faith after the death of his son in an accident, "God's was the first heart to break." This, then, might be the response of God to those who ask, "If the Lord is our shepherd, why do innocent people suffer and die?" God does not, God cannot promise us happy endings in a world where laws of nature and human cruelty take their daily toll. God's promise is not that we will be safe, but that we will never be alone.

Consider once more Jacob's words as he justifies himself to Laban. Note the references to night and darkness toward the end of his remarks, as if he is saying, I can handle things by myself in the daytime. But at night, when darkness takes over my world, life seems ever so much more dangerous and unmanageable. That is when he, and every one of us, needs God to help us make it through the night until dawn breaks again.

And this is the way the psalmist would teach us to see

the world, without illusions that nothing bad will ever happen, but without the fear that we will be utterly destroyed by the things that do happen. We will hurt, but we will heal. We will grieve, but we will grow whole again. Even as the flock needs the shepherd because there are wolves in the world, we will find the world a less frightening and more livable place because "Thou art with me."

CHAPTER THREE

I Shall Not Want

The minister sat by the bed of the desperately ill woman. Modern medicine had done its best, but its best had not been good enough. There would be no miracle. All anyone could do now was ease her pain and try to keep her comfortable until the end came. Having no words of his own for her, the minister opened his Bible, reached out to take her hand, and began to recite the Twenty-third Psalm: "The Lord is my shepherd, I shall not want." The woman's eyes flickered open for a moment as she summoned up the energy to whisper, "But pastor, I do want!"

Of course she wants. She wants to be healthy. She wants to be free of pain. She wants to live long enough to see her grandchildren grow up and marry. These are all perfectly understandable desires. They are the pure, deep longings of her soul, and it grieves her deeply that she will never have them.

We all want things. Is the psalm suggesting that if we have enough faith in God, that will extinguish all desire and we will be content with what we have and long for nothing more? There are some religions, and some voices in every religion, that teach renunciation as the key to happiness in life. Desire nothing and you will never miss anything you don't have. Love no one and no one will have the power to hurt you by leaving you. Teach yourself not to love life too much and death will hold no terror for you. Is this what our psalm is suggesting?

The problem is partly one of translation. The four-hundred-year-old King James translation of the Bible uses words that mean something different in twenty-first-century English than they did in the late sixteenth century. The intent of the Hebrew is more accurately captured by some more recent translations, with words like "I shall lack for nothing." That is, God will provide me with everything I need. Or as a colleague of mine beautifully rendered it, "The Lord is my shepherd, what more do I need?" The issue of whether I desire things beyond that is beside the point.

To want, in Elizabethan English, means not to desire but to lack, to be without something, as in the phrase "to be found wanting" or the poetic line "for want of a nail, a shoe was lost." The promise of the line from the Twenty-third Psalm is that God, our faithful shepherd, will see to it that each member of His flock has enough food and water and a warm, safe place to sleep. An ancient Jewish teaching sees the phrase as having been inspired by the experience of the Israelites wandering in the desert, when God provided for their needs for forty years, supplying them with food, water, even keeping their clothing from wearing out, so that they lacked for nothing.

The message of the psalm would seem to be that, if you don't have something, no matter how much you crave it, you don't really need it. If you needed it, God would have provided you with it. It reminds me of a sign in the window of a general store in a small town I once lived in: "If we don't have it, you're better off without it." It would be saying to people, You have been so seduced by advertising and the consumer culture that you have learned to crave things for which you really have no need. That attitude leaves you in a state of perpetual dissatisfaction, acquisitiveness, and envy of your neighbors. Let us free you from that psychological enslavement and teach you to be content with what you have.

One of the major goals of religion is to teach people to focus gratefully on what they have instead of being aware mostly of what they don't have. Prayers that begin "Thank You for . . ." strike me as more authentically religious than prayers that begin "Please give me . . ." In our society, we have tended to confuse God with Santa Claus and to believe that prayer means making an inventory of everything we would like to have but don't have, and persuading God that we deserve it.

Some readers may be familiar with the song "Unanswered Prayers," popularized by the country music singer Garth Brooks. It tells the story of a man in his mid-forties who sees a woman at a community event who looks vaguely familiar but he can't quite place her. Then he realizes that this is the girl he had a crush on in seventh grade. Every night as a seventh grader, he would go to bed praying to God to make her love him as he loved her, and not understanding why God would not grant the heartfelt prayer of a devout thirteen-year-old boy. Now, thirty years later, seeing who he has grown up to be, seeing who she has grown up to be, he comes to understand that "some of God's greatest gifts are unanswered prayers."

I appreciate the legitimacy, indeed the importance of that message: You will be a happier, more content person if you focus on what God has provided you with, rather than wishing you had more. But at the same time, there is a part of that message that bothers me. I don't like the assertion that God knows what is best for us better than we ourselves do, and that if we really needed what we find ourselves craving, whether health, a job, a loving mate, God would grant our wish, like the wise parent who gives her child the ballet lessons she asks for but refuses to buy her the widely advertised, expensive toy she is crying for. I think that message asks people to deny their feelings, to force themselves not to feel hurt or angry or disappointed, or to pretend that they are not hurt, angry, or disappointed, because they think that is what faith demands of them.

Maybe these words, like the opening line about God being the reliable shepherd/parent who will keep us safe, are really more of a wish than a compliment paid to God. Maybe what we are doing is longing for a life with no more longing, a life in which we will, in fact, lack for nothing because God will have provided us with all we need. When I was studying commentaries on the Psalms as part of the work for my doctorate in Bible, I encountered the term "precative perfect." It is a technical term used by Bible scholars to characterize the partly literary, partly religious technique of wanting something so badly and believing in God's goodness so completely that you picture yourself already having it and thanking God for having given it to you. (Think of the political candidate or Academy Award nominee practicing his acceptance speech long before he knows whether he will win. Think of the high-school girl fantasizing about being married and practicing signing her name "Mrs. [name of schoolmate or rock star she has a crush on].") If we believe that God is good, if we believe that God loves us and has the power to grant our wishes, isn't it reasonable to believe that, even if we don't have something we crave now, we will have it as soon as a busy God, who has a world full of beloved and deserving children to care for, gets around to delivering it? Isn't it a sign of faith in God to say, "I don't have it but I'm sure it's on its way. It's just a matter of time"? The great Protestant theologian Paul Tillich, writing in reference to the messianic hope, offers words that are appropriate to this line from the psalm: "Although waiting is not having, it is also [a kind of] having. The fact that we wait for something shows that in some way we already possess it."

Yes, I have held the hands and dried the tears of people whose marriages had failed or who had been fired from their jobs, and lamented, "Why do I have to go through this? I don't deserve it!" only to hear them tell me two years later that it was the best thing that ever happened to them. They would never have had the nerve to leave a situation that stunted their souls if they had not been pushed, and they were much stronger and happier now. But I have also held the hands and dried the tears of people in hospital rooms who had been told about the incurable illness afflicting them, their child, or their parent and wondered why God was doing this to them. It is hard to say "I shall not want/I shall lack for nothing" at a time like that.

Perhaps we need to ask ourselves, Which is the greater faith: to love God because He gives us everything we ask for, or to love God because He is God, even if life turns out to be less full of blessings than we might have hoped? Would we really be happy if we got everything we craved and lacked for nothing?

The Bible, which generally tries not to demand the impossible of us, nonetheless includes as the last of the Ten Commandments "Thou shalt not covet." But who can refrain from coveting, from wishing we had the shiny new car we see parked across the street or the polite, gifted children who live next door? One interpretation sees those words not as a prohibition but as a promise: Obey these first nine laws, live by God's ways, and your reward will be that you will feel so richly blessed that you will not envy what your neighbor has.

Part of me responds favorably to that interpretation, because I know the power of envy to drain the joy out of the life of even the most successful and richly rewarded person. I remember Peter Shaffer's play, later an Academy Award–winning movie, *Amadeus,* about the life of Mozart, and how his contemporaries could not enjoy their own considerable success or take pleasure in their own significant talent because Mozart had more.

But at the same time, I find myself asking whether not wanting more than you have been given is really a desirable goal for the religiously serious person. If "more" means only more wealth, more fame, more power over other people, a new car, a bigger yacht, then maybe we should pray for the peace of soul that frees us from coveting. But what if the "more" we long for is more wisdom, more generosity, more courage, more wholeness? In a sense, the person who has everything and lacks nothing is missing something very important in life. He has nothing to look forward to, nothing to aspire to. He is missing the feeling of longing for something, yearning for something. He is left without dreams. He will never know the joy of being given the perfect present by someone who loves him and knows what he would appreciate even better than he himself does.

There is a part of me that wants to want, despite the words of our psalm. There is a part of me that wants never to be satisfied with who I am and what I have achieved, that yearns to reach higher, to understand more, to write more books not for the fame or the income but for the opportunity to share with others what life has taught me. And I believe that God is speaking to me and through me when I feel that way. I believe that God has planted in every one of us the desire for more, the reluctance to settle for what we have and what we are, with all of its ambivalence. Our challenge is to want more of the right things.

There is a part of me that insists on loving people though I know it makes me vulnerable to the pain of loss, bereavement, and rejection, because my life would be bland and empty without it. There is a part of me that yearns for a better world, a world without war, without fraud or violence, and refuses to accept the idea that this is the way it is, always has been, and always will be.

Perhaps this is the lesson the second line of the psalm would teach us. If there are empty spaces in your life, dreams that never came true, people who were once there but are gone now, the purpose of those empty spaces is not to frustrate you or to brand you as a loser. The empty spaces may be there to give you room to grow, to dream, to yearn, and to teach you to appreciate what you have because it may not have been there yesterday and may not be there tomorrow.

My version of the psalm's second line would read, The Lord is my shepherd; I shall *often* want. I shall yearn, I shall long, I shall aspire. I shall continue to miss the people and the abilities that are taken from my life as loved ones die and skills diminish. I shall probe the empty spaces in my life like a tongue probing a missing tooth. But I will never feel deprived or diminished if I don't get what I yearn for, because I know how blessed I am by what I have.

CHAPTER FOUR

He Makes Me to Lie Down in Green Pastures

A n old joke tells of a father and son going for a walk in the park. The boy asks his father, "Daddy, why is the sky blue?"

The father answers, "What kind of question is that? The sky is blue because it's blue! That's all there is to it."

A moment later, the boy asks, "Daddy, why is the grass green?"

The father answers, "How should I know? Grass is green because that's what color it is. If it weren't green, it wouldn't be grass."

Timidly, the boy asks, "Daddy, do you mind my asking you all these questions?"

To which the father responds, "No, go ahead and ask. How else will you learn?"

But, in fact, we *can* answer the question of why the sky is blue and the grass is green, at least theologically, and the answer is that God created the world so that we would live comfortably in it.

These are the colors of the rainbow from top to bottom, from outside in: violet, indigo, blue, green, yellow, orange, red. To understand how we see colors, we have to remember that light is a form of energy. Light reaches our eyes in waves of different frequencies per second, creating different levels of intensity. For bright colors, red and yellow, the waves are longer and hit the eye with more strength, even as taller, longer ocean waves hit us more forcefully. You may have noticed that rental cars are often white or red rather than darker colors, easier for other drivers to see and avoid accidents. Darker colors, the blues and greens, emit shorter waves and strike the eye more gently.

Bright colors are exciting to the eye, demanding to be noticed. Red has connotations of blood, of passion. When the artist John Singer Sargent painted a portrait of a society woman in a red dress, he was hinting at her passionate nature. In Nathaniel Hawthorne's novel *The Scarlet Letter,* when the community wants to stigmatize Hester Prynne as a woman who cannot control her emotions, they make her wear a bright red letter *A* for adulteress. When the Nazis set out to separate Jews from the rest of the population, they made them wear yellow stars on their clothing so that they would be instantly noticeable.

By contrast, we find less conspicuous colors calming. Hospital rooms used to be painted white, reflecting hospitals' commitment to thorough cleanliness. Then it was discovered that patients fared better if the walls of their rooms were painted pale green or light blue, soothing colors, rather than stark white.

God has colored His world in predominantly calming colors, blue sky, green leaves, blue-green water, brown trees, colors that calm rather than excite. That may explain a phenomenon that has long puzzled me: Why are we so drawn to the mountains and the seashore when we go on vacation? Why can we sit by the side of a lake for an hour or more, just looking at the water, and feel relaxed?

The answer, I think, is that God's world, decorated in blue and green, calms us, gently bathing our eyes with quiet, low-intensity colors. We spend so much of our lives in a man-made environment, with its artificial lighting and artificial heating and cooling, bright neon signs and color television programs, that when we get a day off, a long weekend, a vacation, we instinctively feel the need to find our way to God's world with its more restful palette.

I remember hearing a lecture by a landscape architect who said surveys had shown that the most satisfying view from a patio or picture window was grass leading to water seen through trees. A psychologist, in an article entitled "Why Scenery Makes Us Happy," suggests that such a landscape "fills us with a sense of security, easy access to food and low exposure to predators." When the psalmist thanks God, his faithful shepherd, for making him lie down in green pastures by still waters, he may be thanking Him not only for the food and the pasture, but also for the greenery. After what may have been a tiring day, he has a place to relax that speaks to him of calm and rest. He is grateful for the opportunity to lie down, to stop striving. He understands that if he had to be on the go all day long, as his ancestors had to be when they were slaves in Egypt, he would wear out. He is grateful that his resting place is green and fertile, rather than dry and harsh. These are among the ways in which God adds to our sense of security, providing us with a refuge from a noisy, intrusive world, an alternative to the way we spend so many of our hours.

Some time ago, a few friends and I set ourselves the intellectual puzzle of deciding when the twentieth century began. We were obviously not talking about what the calendar said, but rather about what the single biggest difference was between life in the nineteenth century and life in the twentieth. The suggestion that won the most support was the invention of electricity. (Honorable mention went to the automobile and World War One.) Electricity liberated us from having to regulate our lives by the rhythms of nature, rising at dawn, and lighting a candle or kerosene lantern to find our way to bed after sunset. It let us rule the night as we ruled the day. That ability to summon light and dispel darkness added greatly to our sense of mastery over the world, with good and bad consequences. It led to the radio, phonograph, movies, television, and the fashioning of a popular culture shared by an entire nation. But in the process, it alienated many of us from the natural world. We spend more of our waking hours under bright lights than we do in God's world of blue skies and green grass. Life has become more hectic, and we find ourselves more anxious and emotionally exhausted.

Evan Eisenberg, in his book *The Ecology of Eden,* distinguishes between "mountain cultures" and "tower cultures." In mountain cultures, people live in God's world. They regard the world of nature with reverence, the kind of heart-lifting feeling we get when we gaze at a mountain range. They seek to integrate themselves into God's world. In Psalm 121, the psalmist "lift[s his] eyes unto the hills" and is reminded that God is the source of his help and strength. By contrast, in tower cultures, people live in a man-made environment. They regard nature as raw material awaiting their efforts to reshape and improve it. They spend a great deal of time admiring the work of their own hands, and, as a result, God is hard to find.

For most of the nineteenth century in the United States, people lived in mountain cultures. They worked outdoors, farming, logging, riding from place to place on horseback, surrounded by green trees and fields, blue skies and lakes. They may have found their work physically demanding, but their surroundings served to relax them. There was a calming blandness to the world they saw around them. When they wanted a break from their everyday routines, when they craved excitement and stimulation, I can picture nineteenth-century Americans being attracted to brightly colored spectacles, actors and clowns in red and yellow costumes, exciting acts with fire and wild animals. Then, as the twentieth century progressed, more and more Americans found themselves living in cities, the epitome of tower culture. They lived and worked among tall buildings and in dark factories, with hardly a glimpse of the sky and virtually no grass to be seen. Today we spend our days overwhelmed with stimulation, assaulted by bright lights and loud noises all day long, and when we turn to diversions such as loud, fast-paced television shows, movies filled with explosions and car crashes, there comes a point when they don't please us as they once did. Maybe that's because bright colors and stimulating acts are the last things we need. They may be precisely what we need a break from. Our souls crave the restful blues and greens of the seashore, the lakeside, the forest. That may also explain why so many city dwellers, as soon as they could afford it, fled the cities and took on the burdens and blessings of suburban life, mowing lawns, carpooling their children, and commuting an hour to work, just to live in God's color palette rather than man's.

As many readers may know, Jews celebrate the winter festival of Hanukkah by lighting candles at the darkest time of the year. We light one candle on the first night of the eight-day-long holiday, two on the second, and so on. One December, I received a call from a member of my congregation who told me that she had been given an electric menorah (the Hanukkah candelabra) as a present, one that used lightbulbs instead of candles. She wanted to know if it would be proper to use it for the holiday. I told her that, while electric menorahs are advisable for celebrating Hanukkah in hotel rooms, college dormitories, and other venues where burning candles might be a safety hazard, one does not recite the traditional Hanukkah blessings over a lightbulb. To turn on an electric light is to be in the presence of a human artifact. To kindle a fire, to light a candle, is to be in the presence of one of God's gifts to the world.

In much the same way, to work in an air-conditioned, all-electric office is to inhabit a world that is the product of human minds and hands. I appreciate the comfort, but I must remember that it takes me out of the world God created, and I lose something precious in the exchange. To lie down in green pastures is to live in God's world. The noise of car horns and fire engines keeps us awake at night. The sound of crickets chirping and waves lapping the shore lulls us to sleep.

So why is the sky blue? Why is the grass green? One answer is that God in His wisdom anticipated a time when people would be overstimulated by bright lights and loud colors, and He provided us with an escape from all that stimulation, a world fashioned in colors that relax the eye and the soul. When we are exhausted by the strains of living in an artificial world, when we crave the peace and serenity that the psalmist knew and cherished, undisturbed by the noise of automobiles and the blare of television laugh tracks, we know where to find it. God has given us green pastures to lie down in, green trees for us to gaze at, a blue sky to lift our souls. And we should thank Him for it.

CHAPTER FIVE

He Leads Me Beside the Still Waters

Water is life. We are nurtured in water before we are born. Our bodies are mostly water. We can go without food far longer than we can go without water. I have known the feeling of moderate dehydration when I have neglected to drink water during a hike, a long plane ride, or a strenuous exercise session, and I know how unsettling that feeling can be. An episode of the television drama series *ER* included a vignette of an elderly nursing-home resident, neglected by an overworked staff, who becomes irrational as a result of dehydration, attacks a policeman with his own gun, and is shot and killed, all for lack of water. Scientists looking for the possibility of life on other planets look first for evidence of water. There can be no life without water.

In the part of the world where the Bible was written, the climate is different than it is in the temperate United States and Europe. There are only two seasons, six months during which it rains more or less regularly (unless there is a periodic drought) and six months during which the skies are cloudless and no rain falls. This is the part of the world that gave rise to the myth of Tammuz, the fertility god who dies in the spring and is resurrected in the fall, and to the story of Persephone. In that Greek tale, Persephone, daughter of the goddess of agriculture, is kidnapped by Hades, lord of the underworld. To compel Hades to release her, her mother makes the crops stop growing. Hades is forced to compromise by letting Persephone return to earth for half the year (the half when rain will be allowed to fall and crops to grow) and spend the other half of the year (the arid months) with him. And this is the part of the world where, as I learned when I was living in Israel, the radio and television news programs stop giving weather forecasts after May 1 because every day's weather will be the same, sunny and hot under cloudless skies.

In those conditions, water is life not only for the individual but for the community. Rain is not just something that cancels picnics and inconveniences shoppers, as we experience it today. Rain replenishes the moisture in the soil and lets the crops grow, giving people and their animals something to eat. Think of all the biblical stories that begin "Now there was a famine in the land. . . ." The first great empires in human history grew up around the Nile River in Egypt and the Tigris and Euphrates Rivers in the land that was sequentially called Mesopotamia ("the land between the rivers"), Assyria, and Babylonia, and is now known as Iraq. Before the great rulers of ancient times controlled armies, they controlled rivers and distributed the water that made the crops grow. So when the psalmist thanks his faithful shepherd for leading him to water, it is more than thirst-quenching refreshment for which he is grateful. It is life itself.

But if water is the stuff of life, it can also be the cause of death. People drown in water. People drive off bridges into rivers or are swept away by floods. Monsoons regularly kill people by the tens of thousands in the Indian subcontinent. A little bit of water refreshes us; too much water frightens us.

Though zoologists tell us that life began in water and only later emerged onto dry land, we humans are much more comfortable on land than we are in the water. We are constantly aware that we can't breathe underwater. We are uneasy when our feet can't touch the bottom of the pool or pond. We are anxious at sea, out of sight of land, when we don't know where we are, find distances impossible to estimate, and need compass-reading skills to know in which direction to steer. At some level, our discomfort in the water may be more than a realistic fear of drowning. It may be an ancient fear that the water we once lived in is coming back to reclaim us.

In olden times, people who lived by the ocean would watch the waves coming in, reaching higher and higher on the shoreline. It might well have seemed to them that the water was trying to take over the land. They told stories like the tale of Noah's Ark and parallel accounts of a great flood in other cultures. And lest we think those are only the irrational fears of ignorant, prescientific people who did not understand the ways of the tides, newspapers and magazines in recent years have carried stories of beach erosion on the Maine and Massachusetts coasts, endangering homes built close to the ocean, and of the threat of global warming melting the polar ice caps and raising the ocean level until cities in Florida and along the Gulf Coast find themselves inundated. The waters from which we emerged millions of years ago may indeed be coming back to reclaim us.

On the opening page of the Bible, the first thing God does is create light and separate light from darkness. Then the second thing God does, and I bet you never noticed that it takes Him a day and a half to do it (Genesis 1:6–10), longer than it takes Him to do anything else that week, is to mop up all the water that dominates His creation, turning some of it into clouds and the rest into oceans, so that dry land can appear. For the men and women of the biblical world, dry land represented the opportunity to control what happens. Water is chaos. In Genesis 49:4, the patriarch Jacob criticizes his eldest son, Reuben, for being "as unstable as water." The prophet Jeremiah, seeking to persuade Israel of the power and goodness of God, praises God as One "who set the sand as a boundary to the sea, as a limit for all time. . . . Though its waves toss, though they roar, they cannot pass it" (Jeremiah 5:22). When God responds to Job's challenge in chapter thirty-eight of the Book of Job and asks, "Where were you when I laid the earth's foundations?" He goes on to say, "Who closed the sea behind doors . . . when I make breakers My limit for it, saying You may come so far and no further; here your surging waves must stop." And in the New Testament (Matthew 8:23–27), Jesus demonstrates his special powers by calming a "great storm in the sea."

Modern men and women understand that water is not all that chaotic. It always flows from higher ground to lower. It always freezes at thirty-two degrees Fahrenheit. An experienced sailor can find his way in the ocean more easily than I can navigate the streets of downtown Boston. But to the biblical mind, water was unpredictable, threatening to overflow its bounds and reclaim the land it once covered. Storms, floods, surging tides were frightening. God was not only the source of the water without which we could not live, sending the rain in its season. God was the power that controlled all that water, setting limits to the tides, keeping us safe from the flood. God's promise to Noah (Genesis 9:11) was that "never again will there be a flood to destroy the earth." He set the rainbow in the heavens as a reminder of His promise that, no matter how hard it rained, sooner or later the rain would stop and the sun would come out again.

If, as I have suggested, the Twenty-third Psalm is in part a song of praise to God for helping us feel safe in an unsafe world, the line about the still waters adds another dimension to that feeling of security. God is the one who gives us water so that we can live, but at the same time makes sure that there is not too much water so that life becomes difficult. There is a prayer in the Jewish liturgical tradition, to be recited in the early fall when the rainy season begins in Israel, that asks God to send abundant rain but not too much rain, that it be "a blessing and not a curse."

There are two ways of imagining God's creative activity at the beginning of time and in the opening pages of the Bible. We can believe that in the beginning there was nothing and God called everything that is into existence: Let there be dry land and seas, let there be trees and grass, let there be birds and fish and beasts. Or we can believe that in the beginning there was everything but it was all mixed up, and God fashioned a world by sorting out the mess, separating earth from sky, dry land from water, decreeing that every species of plant and animal reproduce after its own kind. I am inclined to favor the second approach. Creativity as I like to think of it does not necessarily mean making something out of nothing. The creative poet does not coin new words; he arranges existing words in a way that no one ever did before. The creative scientist or historian does not make things up; that is the opposite of good scientific or academic practice. He or she identifies patterns that had not been previously noted. And I see God creating a world not by making earth and water appear in what had been empty space, but by sorting out the earth and the sea, setting bounds for the water and letting the dry land appear. God is the power that imposes order on chaos so that the world is livable. God's power keeps the force of gravity constant so that objects don't float away when we reach for them, so that the walls of our homes stand upright. God's power keeps all the laws of physics and chemistry constant so that we can count on foods and medicines doing what they are supposed to do.

Newton's second law of thermodynamics, the law of entropy, tells us that a system left to itself will move over time from order to chaos. Leave an automobile in a field outdoors for several months and it will become a heap of rusty metal. But a heap of rusty metal left outdoors will never turn into an automobile. It takes deliberate intervention to turn sheets of metal into a car. One of God's gifts to us, then, is that the world is not left unattended to run down over time. Though it has been around for billions of years, it has not reverted to chaos because God keeps it orderly. Even the floods and earthquakes, though they strike us as random and unpredictable, are obeying firmly established laws of nature.

In an earlier book I wrote of a conversation I had with a friend of mine, who is a physicist, about whether Newton's second law, the tendency toward chaos, was an argument for or against the existence of God. A biologist wrote to me and said that, had I spoken to a biologist rather than a physicist, the case for God would have been stronger. Maybe in the world of physics, order reverts to chaos. A jar of marbles carefully sorted by size and color becomes hopelessly jumbled when you shake it a few times. But consider the growth of a human fetus, my correspondent wrote. It starts out as a cluster of undifferentiated cells, and over the course of a few months, by a process that should never cease to astonish us no matter how many millions of times it happens, some of those cells become eyes, some become lungs, some become fingers. Randomness gives way to order. Isn't that God at work?

If we extend the contrast between still water and surging water from the natural to the emotional realm, we can see God as the power that lets us control all the surging emotions that well up inside each of us. Many of us have known the experience of having emotions get out of control, and we know what a frightening, unsettling experience that can be, like being in the path of a flood. In the midst of an argument, a man loses his temper and lashes out at his neighbor, using words or even fists in a way that he will be ashamed of for a long time. A woman who sincerely believes that her future happiness depends on her losing weight and becoming more attractive finds she cannot stop herself from reaching for the pint of ice cream or the box of cookies to fill the emotional void inside her, and she hates herself for her weakness. A happily married man or woman notices an attractive colleague at work. Soon, an innocent flirtation becomes an intense friendship and drifts into a sexual affair, something neither party believes in or was really looking for. Sexual passion is a good thing; the human race would have died out long ago without it. In the same way, a capacity for outrage when we have been offended and an ability to enjoy good food are desirable qualities of the human spirit. But like the river that overflows its banks and destroys the homes it had given life to, these desirable instincts can surge out of control and destroy our lives.

At that point, God becomes the power that enables us to control the out-of-control feelings. It is God who "closes the [emotional] sea behind doors, saying 'Here your surging waves will stop.' " What are the twelve-step programs—for alcoholics, drug addicts, compulsive overeaters—if not invitations to God, one's Higher Power, to help a person do what he or she has not been able to do alone, to set limits on instinctual drives that threaten to get out of control and ruin one's life? I have spoken to people involved in twelve-step programs and they have told me of the terrifying feeling of not being able to stop themselves from doing something that they know is wrong and will turn their life into chaos. It is like being in the path of a flood and being swept away by raging waters.

When the psalmist praises God for leading him beside the still waters, he is not only thanking God for providing him with refreshing water to quench his thirst. He is thanking God for keeping the waters still, keeping them manageable and less threatening. He is thanking God for the blessing of self-control.

This is something that religion does that even ostensibly religious people don't always appreciate. It sets limits. It tells us that sometimes too much of a good thing—food, wine, sex, the desire to succeed in business—is no longer a good thing. There are even limits to how much time one should spend with family and how much of one's income a person should give to charity. We need not dismiss or repress any of those things as bad just because they can be done to excess. The God who set limits to the ocean waves, the God who promised Noah that the rain would never again cover the whole earth and wipe out all life, has set limits to the surging drives within each of us, saying, This far shall you go and no further, and if you cannot stop yourself, call on Me and let Me help you.

This is the lesson the psalmist would convey to us when he speaks of being led by still waters. This is the divine gift to which it points. If you have ever known the terrifying feeling of not being able to control your emotions, be reassured that there is a God in the world to help you control them.

Several years ago, I was sitting in a television studio, waiting to be interviewed about a book I had written on the power of religion to make us feel cleansed and forgiven, when one of the cameramen took me aside to tell me that the most authentic religious experiences he ever has come not in the church sanctuary on Sunday morning but in the church basement on Tuesday evening when he attends the weekly meeting of his Alcoholics Anonymous support group. He said to me, "It's exactly what you write about. For years, I tried to stop drinking, and it never worked. I had about given up on myself as someone too weak to do what I needed to do. I knew I was hurting my family, but I thought I couldn't help myself. Then I joined AA. They taught me to ask God to share His strength with me so I could do with Him what I could never do alone. I haven't had a drink in almost two years, and, believe me, I thank God every morning for that."

Why do we need God to help us do something we can't do by or for ourselves? My friend and colleague Rabbi Joseph Telushkin offers this analogy: He knows people who are dieting to lose weight, who sincerely want to lose weight, but often give in to temptation "just this once" or on special occasions or when they are upset or feeling sorry for themselves or when they are drawn to the coffee and doughnuts in cold weather or the ice cream cone in hot weather. He also knows people, sometimes the same people, observant Jews committed to the Jewish dietary laws, who will go hungry if an airline has neglected to take on board their special meal or if they attend a reception at which there is no food they can eat. Temptation never seems to get the better of them. Why? Because we take commitments to God more seriously than we take promises to ourselves. Because doing something with God is easier than doing it alone.

In Hebrew, the term for "still waters" is *mei menuhot,* waters of rest and relaxation. We can relax, confident in our abilities to control those restless impulses within us because God is on our side, bringing order where there would otherwise be chaos and giving us rest.

CHAPTER SIX

He Restores My Soul

Every morning shortly after awakening, a traditional Jew recites this prayer: "The soul that You have given me, O God, is pure. You fashioned it, You breathed it into me, You keep body and soul together. One day You will take it from me, only to restore it to me in time to come. So long as I have my soul, I must acknowledge You as my God and the God of my ancestors, the God of all souls. Praised are You O Lord *who restores the soul to a lifeless body*" (italics added).

What is a soul? Let me suggest that a soul is what people have that animals don't. It represents everything that elevates human beings and brings us closer to God. Animals can be brave and loyal. They can be devoted parents. They can feel sad when a member of their group dies. But even the most dedicated advocate of the emotional wisdom of animals would have to admit that there is a range of behavior, having to do with moral choices, of which animals are incapable. They can be obedient, they can be helpful, but they cannot be good in a moral sense. "Good doggie" is no more a moral statement than "good weather," and the dog that knocks over the lamp, like the tiger that kills the only doctor in the village, is not being bad in moral terms. I think that is what the Bible is hinting at when it describes God as creating the animals by saying "Let there be . . ." but creating the first humans by breathing something of Himself into them (as the prayer I quoted alludes to). It is that little bit of God within each of us that makes us capable of *choosing* to be good, choosing to be generous, choosing to be forgiving. Only creatures with souls can do that.

And that is why the worshiper understands that "as long as I have my soul, I must acknowledge You as my God." As far as we know, no animal could understand, let alone offer, that prayer.

When a worshiper praises God for "restoring the soul to a lifeless body," he or she is not speaking of a future resurrection. The worshiper is responding to the miraculous experience of waking up in the morning. When we are asleep, it is as if we have no soul. We are not doing anything uniquely human. Only when we wake up do we again don the mantle of humanity, capable of moral decisions.

To the ancient mind, sleep must have seemed like an anticipation of death (or perhaps death was seen as a permanent state of sleep). The worshiper reciting the prayer I cited is saying, in effect, I'm alive again. I survived the night. My mind and body are functioning normally. I have an awareness of myself as a human being, facing a new day with its myriad opportunities to do human things, to love, to learn, to help others. Thank God for that.

The Ninety-second Psalm is another of my favorites. It urges us to have faith in God's goodness even when life seems unfair, assuring us that, though "the wicked may spring up as grass," they will soon wither, while "the righteous shall flourish like a palm tree and grow mighty like a cedar of Lebanon." The opening lines of the Ninety-second Psalm read:

> It is good to praise the Lord,
> To sing hymns to Your name, O Most High,
> To proclaim your lovingkindness in the morning
> And your faithfulness at night.

Reflecting on those opening lines, one commentator suggests that we experience God's lovingkindness, God's giving us gifts we have no right or power to demand from Him, when we wake up each morning from the mini-death that is sleep and discover that we are still alive and well; God has restored our souls to us. And we experience God's faithfulness, His reliability, at night when we give ourselves leave to go to sleep, relying on God to keep the world intact while we let ourselves ignore it and to ensure that our world will still be there when we wake up in the morning.

Are there other circumstances when, like the sleeper, we are not doing anything uniquely human, so that it is as if we had no soul? I read once of a group of tourists on safari in Africa. They had hired several native porters to carry their supplies while they trekked. After three days, the porters told them that they would have to stop and rest for a day. They were not tired, they explained, but "we have walked too far too fast and now we must wait for our souls to catch up to us."

We too can be so busy taking care of things that we neglect our souls. What shall we say about the men and women who invest so much time and energy in their jobs that they have neither time nor energy left for their families when they arrive home? Do they need to pause to let their souls catch up to them? What shall we say about the person who exaggerates the virtues of his product or uses technical jargon to confuse a customer in order to close a sale, except to suspect that he may have lost his soul? And what about the CEO who "downsizes" his workforce, rendering hundreds, even thousands, of people unemployed, every four people now required to do the work of five, not because it will improve efficiency or eliminate duplication but solely to enhance the price of a share of his company's stock and substantially increase his own income? Perhaps the kindest thing we can say is that he needs to have his soul restored. A member of my congregation told me of how he was ordered to reduce the number of employees in his department by one-fourth, and how he could not sleep for a week in anticipation of having to tell people who had worked faithfully for him that they would no longer have a job. I told him that I appreciated how hard it must have been for him, and he answered that it would have been worse had he been able to carry out the order without feeling pain. It was better to lose sleep than to lose one's soul.

When our work compels us (or when we think it compels us) to repress what God has planted in us of Himself, so that we see other people as competitors, as threats to our success, our language betrays the fact that we have lost our souls. We plead "it's a jungle out there" and describe it as a "dog-eat-dog world," a world in which we have no use for the qualities that make us different from animals.

The world asks so much of us. We give ourselves so totally to our work, to the task of raising our family and running a home, to our volunteer commitments that we often forget to take time to nourish our souls, forgetting that we need to rely on the wisdom of the soul to guide our working and our living hours. Our bodies are more active when we are awake than when we are sleeping, sometimes frantically so. But our souls may be as absent during the day as they are at night. We lack the wisdom of those native porters, the wisdom to know that we have left our souls behind and we need to stop and let our souls catch up to us. The psalmist would remind us that God has given us ways to reclaim our humanity when pressures of time and obligation have caused us to misplace it, and that part of God's role as faithful guardian of the flock is to urge us to remember to be human. Our task is to stop long enough to hear that message.

The Bible thought that the need to have God restore our souls was so important that it listed the Sabbath as a day of rest as one of the Ten Commandments, along with the obligation to honor one's parents and the forbidding of murder and adultery. (Old Jewish joke: The rabbi in his sermon points to the Ten Commandments on the synagogue wall and says, "You see, according to the Bible, working on the Sabbath is exactly the same as committing adultery." At which point a congregant calls out, "I don't know about you, Rabbi, but I'm in a position to say that they're not the same at all.") The biblical Sabbath is not primarily a day of rules and prohibitions, though it has often been misunderstood to be just that. I have read about communities where people were fined and punished for laughing on Sunday, the Christian Sabbath, or scolded for wearing comfortable clothes instead of suits and dresses. And growing up in Brooklyn, I knew observant Jewish girls who "honored" the Sabbath by spending the last two hours of a Saturday afternoon watching the clock, waiting impatiently for the Sabbath to end so that they could wash their hair before going on a date.

But I would insist that those are misunderstandings of the Bible's intent. The Sabbath was given to us as a gift, not as a penalty. The people to whom it was first given had grown up as slaves in Egypt. God said to them, When you were slaves, someone else owned your time. You could do only what they told you to do. Now that you are free, you can use your time for your own purposes. That is why, to this day, three thousand years after the event, a Jewish family welcoming the Sabbath refers to it as "a reminder of our liberation from Egyptian slavery."

Animals are controlled by time. Some sleep at night and hunt for food by day, while others reverse the cycle, but they have no choice in the matter. Animals mate only when the season calls for a female to come into heat. Human beings, and only human beings, control time. We can work late, or we can take a day off. We can make love to express intimacy, not because the season commands us to. If, during the week, a man or woman is bound to a schedule, if our lives are ruled by the clock so that we are not free to do what we want when we want to, the Sabbath (whether observed on Saturday, Sunday, or even on a weekday for those who have to work weekends) is a day to replenish our souls by being free to do those things that identify us as human. It is a time for family, for reading, and of course for worship, another uniquely human activity.

Families whose members are too busy to sit down for a meal at the same time during the week would do well to make a point of eating together at least once or twice every weekend. I was astonished to read of the difference it makes to a child's or an adolescent's sense of rootedness to share mealtime with his or her parents.

I recently got into a conversation with a man who asked what I do for a living. When I told him I write books, he said, "I wish I had time to read a book. My wife reads all the time. It gives her a lot of pleasure, and she learns a lot about human nature from her reading. But I'm just too busy." I too wish he had time to read. He deserves the kind of break from his working schedule that reading represents. As a uniquely human activity, it would nourish a part of his soul that he is currently neglecting.

Best-selling author Herman Wouk recalls the time his novel *The Caine Mutiny* was being turned into a Broadway play, and he was an adviser to the project. A week before opening night, dialogue was being rewritten and scenes had to be restaged. Late Friday afternoon, Wouk, an observant Jew, told the director that he was leaving for the Sabbath and would return in twenty-four hours. The director was beside himself, explaining that this was a critical time for a play in which people had invested tens of thousands of dollars, but Wouk was adamant. He returned a day later, refreshed and able to make suggestions that people who had been working nonstop had never thought of.

I can relate to that. When one of my books is published, I embark on an extended promotional tour to publicize it. But I insist on being home for the Sabbath every week. It rules out some cities and causes me to turn down some attractive invitations, but especially when I am most busy, I need to define myself by something other than my work, lest I lose part of my soul in the process.

Do you know who was the first to replenish his soul on the Sabbath? God Himself. In the Book of Exodus, we read, "You shall keep My Sabbaths, for this is a sign between Me and you throughout the generations . . . that in six days the Lord made heaven and earth and on the seventh day He rested and was refreshed" (Exodus 31:13, 17). In Hebrew, the verbs referring to God's resting and being refreshed are *shavat,* "He stopped," from which we get the word "Sabbath," and *yinafash,* literally "He got His soul back."

If we put our soul into our work, if, rather than just going through the motions, what we do flows from the deepest part of our being, then after a burst of creativity, we need to replenish our souls. If we only put forth and never take in, eventually we will run dry. Even God had to pause after a creative effort to let His soul be restored.

I can imagine that something similar holds true for a woman who has given birth to a child. To bring a living soul into the world is probably the most creative thing anyone will ever do. When Eve gives birth to Cain, she exclaims, "Like God, I have made a person!" (Genesis 4:1). Just as nurturing the child within her for nine months draws on the mother's physical resources, giving that child a soul draws on her spiritual resources. It would make sense for a new mother, despite all that a newborn infant demands of her, to take time to replenish her soul in the weeks after the birth, even as God did after creating the first human beings, to ensure that she will have the depth of soul to be a good parent. This might mean staying home from work for several weeks, not only for the infant's sake but for her own. It might mean hiring someone to help with household chores so that she will have time to read or listen to music. Her soul needs to recuperate from the process of having a child even as her body does.

And at the other end of the life cycle, when someone close to us dies and we feel empty inside, we need God and we need other people to fill the void, to assure us that our loved one is still with us in some very important ways. If God cannot restore the soul of the one who died, if God cannot bring the person back to life, He can do much to replenish the souls of those who grieve.

When we lose someone we love, when death, divorce, or other circumstances separate us from a "soul mate," we feel that our souls have been diminished. Human souls are nourished by love, by relationships, and to sever a relationship is to chip away at a person's soul. That is why we need prayer and healing, mediated through friends and other good people, to "restore our souls." Whether we believe that we will be reunited with our loved one in a time and place to come, or whether we believe that we keep a person close to us by cherishing that person's values and memories, our religious faith helps us to fill the emptiness. You don't have to be religious to have a soul; everybody has one. You don't have to be religious to perfect your soul; I have found saintliness in avowed atheists. But maybe you have to be religious to have your soul restored. The prophet Jeremiah compares the person who scorns and rejects God to a tree planted in the desert, which will ultimately dry up and wither because it has no source of replenishment outside itself, while "he who trusts in the Lord . . . shall be like a tree planted by waters . . . its leaves are ever fresh, it has no care in a year of drought, it does not cease to bear fruit" (Jeremiah 17:7–8). When we are emotionally empty, we are not able to replenish ourselves. The restoration, the replenishment has to come from somewhere outside ourselves, from God and from people inspired by God to reach out to us in our need.

Should you know someone who has suffered a loss, whether loss of a loved one, loss of a job, or loss of a relationship, and you hesitate to contact your friend because you feel inadequate to the situation, because you are not sure you have the words to help her, please overcome that hesitation and reach out to your friend. Call her, visit her. You don't have to say anything besides "I'm sorry, I feel bad for you." Human souls are nourished by relationships, and your friendship, your going out of your way to show concern, has the power to heal a person's soul.

There is one other important way in which God restores our souls when they verge on wearing thin. As many readers may be aware, my wife and I had a fourteen-year-old son who died of progeria, the extremely rare rapid-aging disease. Almost exactly two years after his death, our daughter reached the age of becoming Bat Mitzvah and was preparing to celebrate that status by reading from the Torah and the prophets at a Sabbath service. As luck would have it, on the Sabbath closest to her thirteenth birthday, the Jewish liturgical calendar called for her to chant the fortieth chapter of Isaiah, concluding with the words, "Those who trust in the Lord will have their strength renewed. They shall mount up with wings as angels. They shall run and not grow weary, they shall walk and not feel faint" (Isaiah 40:31).

Our family fastened on those words as a statement of what had happened to us during those two years, of how we had survived our son's and brother's death with our faith strong and our ability to celebrate life intact. We had come to the conclusion that God was not responsible for Aaron's death; genetics had caused it. God's role was not to send the tragedy into our lives for reasons that surpassed human understanding. God's role was to send us the spiritual resources to go on living in an unfair and often painful world. How else does one manage to keep running and not grow weary, unless the words of Isaiah are true and God is there to renew our strength? We realized that we had walked the same path as the author of the Twenty-third Psalm, starting in the valley of the shadow of death and slowly, step after step, finding our way through the valley until we found the waiting world of sunlight.

And I have seen dozens, even hundreds, of instances in which the prophet's words proved true: the parents who, more than twenty years ago, gave birth to a severely brain-damaged child and against the advice of doctors and relatives took him home and cared for him day after day, year after year; the woman who, three times a week, goes to the nursing home to visit her elderly mother who is afflicted with Alzheimer's disease and cannot recognize her; the husband who faithfully tends to his wife as she loses ground to a degenerative disease and who speaks to me only of her pain and her courage, never of the burden it places on him. Had you asked these people five years ago, twenty-five years ago, if they thought they were capable of such devotion for so long, I suspect that each of them would have said, I hope I never have to find out if I am, because I fear it is more than I could handle. Where do people get the strength to be so caring, so compassionate, so human in the best sense of the word, if not from a God who renews their strength, who restores their soul when they have depleted their soul, so that they can do what they know is the right thing, even if it is the difficult thing, to do? If depression is the "dark night of the soul," God is the magnetic force that guides people through the dark night and brings them into a brighter world.

I am often invited to speak to conferences of doctors, nurses, hospice workers, or schoolteachers. When I do, I always save the last ten minutes of my remarks to address the problem of "caregiver burnout," the fatigue and depression that is too often the result of caring for the emotionally needy. I tell my audiences not to be afraid to love their patients, their students, not to be afraid to enter into their pain, out of concern that they will exhaust their own emotional resources and have nothing left for others in their care, let alone for their own families. I assure them that love and strength are not like bank accounts that grow smaller as you use them. They are like muscles that grow stronger with use. And I urge them to rely on God to renew their strength so that they can go on working and not grow weary.

When we have poured out all the love and all the strength we have on behalf of people who need our love and our strength, when we have spent ourselves holding the hands of the fearful and drying the tears of the grieving, when we have labored to feed the hungry, clothe the naked, and build homes for the homeless, and, despite our efforts, the problems are still there, where do we find the strength to go on?

When our souls are on the verge of giving in to compassion fatigue, when we know what the right thing to do is but we are tired of being charitable and helpful, that is when we need God to restore our souls, to replenish our ability to act like human beings, to understand that what is asked of us is not to make the world perfect but to make one person's life better. When events challenge our faith so that we find it hard to believe that this world is God's world, that is when we need God to restore our souls, to reinforce our ability to believe in ourselves and in our ability to do good things. Even as a faithful shepherd gives his flock the food and water they need to be sheep, God, our faithful shepherd, gives us the strength of soul we need to be human.

CHAPTER SEVEN

He Guides Me in Straight Paths for His Name's Sake

There is a story in the Talmud about the traveler who asks a child, "Is there a shortcut to such-and-such a village?" The child answers, "There is a shortcut that is long and a long way that is short." The story comes to mind as I contemplate this verse from the Twenty-third Psalm because the Hebrew phrase translated "straight paths" actually says something more complex and more interesting than the translation would convey. It literally means "roundabout ways that end up in the right direction."

I can relate to that. I suspect we have all had the experience of trying to take a shortcut, whether while driving or in other aspects of our lives, and finding ourselves entangled in a mess we would have done well to avoid. When it comes to our health, our education, or the forging of personal relationships, we are so often in a hurry to get to where we want to end up that we take shortcuts and end up regretting it. How often have we said to our doctor, our accountant, or our clergyman, "Do I really have to go to all this trouble? Isn't there an easier way to accomplish this?" And the answer has been virtually the same one as the child gave the traveler: "Yes, there are shortcuts but they will end up being longer, harder, and more expensive in the end." I can't count the number of times someone has told me at a funeral, "Rabbi, I don't see the need to take off all those days for the traditional seven-day memorial week. A day or two should be enough. I'm a busy person." And I have had to warn those people that if they try to rush through the grieving process, they will end up spending more time with me or with a therapist, trying to deal with the undigested lump of grief in their hearts, than they will save by taking the shortcut.

Maybe in plane geometry the shortest distance between two points is a straight line. But in life the shortest distance to our goal may be an indirect, roundabout route. The straight line between us and our goal may have hidden traps or land mines, or it may be too easy and never challenge us to discover our strengths or give us time to let those strengths emerge. When the Israelites left Egypt, we read that God did not lead them on the most direct route to the Promised Land precisely because it was short (Exodus 13:17). They needed extra travel time to make the transition from having been slaves to being a free people. The young woman who is the narrator of the biblical love poem *The Song of Songs* has to warn her lover three times not to rush things; "do not stir or awaken love until it pleases," that is, until the right time. The promising baseball player to whom success has always come easily may have to fail and go back to the minor leagues to learn to cope with adversity. A person may go through two or three careers early in life before she discovers what she really wants to do, and will find the experience of those early dead ends indispensable to her ultimate success. We may be reluctant to take a vacation because of problems at work, only to find that a book we read or a person we meet on vacation turns out to offer us the solution to our problem. And when that happens, I hope we will remember to thank God for having led us in *ma'aglei tzedek,* roundabout paths that finally brought us to where we were meant to end up. Once again, it is when we find the world baffling and frustrating that God inspires us and helps make life more satisfying.

But what does it mean to say that God does that, or anything else, "for His name's sake"? Some modern translations are so uncomfortable with the notion of God doing something primarily to make Himself look good that they resort to tampering with the familiar and well-loved version of the psalm, translating the line "He guides me by true paths as He Himself is true" (Rev. James Moffatt); "He guides me in right paths as befits His name" (Jewish Publication Society); "He guides me on the paths of righteousness so that I may serve Him with love" (the gifted poet Stephen Mitchell). After all, aren't we inclined to think less of a person who gives charity or is active in church "for his name's sake," solely in order to enhance his reputation? How can we attribute similar motivation to God?

Perhaps we can gain insight as to what the psalmist is saying by examining another problematic biblical passage. When God sends Moses to demand that Pharaoh free the Hebrew slaves, God tells him, "I will harden Pharaoh's heart . . . and the Egyptians shall know that I am the Lord when I stretch out My hand over Egypt and bring the Israelites out of their midst" (Exodus 7:3–5). The Ten Plagues follow, with Pharaoh agreeing each time to free the slaves and then changing his mind. Many a reader has been troubled by the apparent unfairness of God causing Pharaoh to be stubborn and then punishing him for his stubbornness. It raises questions as to whether God is just and whether people are responsible for their actions. If Pharaoh couldn't help being cruel and stubborn, if his being cruel and stubborn was part of God's stage-managing the drama, why should he be punished for it?

The medieval Jewish philosopher Maimonides and the twentieth-century psychologist Erich Fromm both offer the same explanation. Carefully reading the story of the plagues in Exodus, both note that for the first five plagues, the Bible speaks of Pharaoh hardening *his own* heart. Only for the last five does God harden Pharaoh's heart. The implication is that in the beginning, Pharaoh's decision, though it could have been predicted, was still his free choice. He could have chosen to free the slaves; he decided not to. And each time he repeated that choice, it became a little bit less of a free choice and more of a habit. That is what the Bible is saying when it tells us that God hardened Pharaoh's heart. God made the human soul in such a way that, when we repeatedly do something, whether good or bad, it becomes part of our character.

Fromm writes: "Every evil act tends to harden a man's heart, that is, to deaden it. Every good deed tends to soften it, to make it more alive. The more man's heart hardens, the less freedom does he have to change, the more is he determined already by previous action. But there comes a point of no return when man's heart has become so hardened and so deadened that he has lost the possibility of freedom."* In other words, God doesn't take away Pharaoh's freedom to choose between good and evil, between compassion and cruelty. Pharaoh himself gives that freedom away by repeatedly choosing evil until he has defined himself in his own mind as a person who always makes the cruel choice. Even as my computer recognizes patterns I have followed before, so that I need type only the first two letters of a website or e-mail address before the computer assumes I am doing something I have

*Erich Fromm, *You Shall Be as Gods* (Greenwich, Conn.: Fawcett, 1966), p. 81.

done before, God has built into the human soul a kind of "feedback recognition mechanism" in such a way that every time we do something good, we make it easier to do good again because we have come to think of ourselves as someone who acts that way, and every time we do something wrong, we make it more likely that we will choose that same wrong path again.

But if God can foresee that Pharaoh will repeatedly refuse to free the Hebrew slaves, why go through the charade of making him promise and then predictably break his promise? Why not send the last and most overwhelming plague right away instead of making people suffer through plagues that God knows will be ineffective? The answer lies in God's words to Moses: "and the Egyptians shall know that I am the Lord."

Does it really matter who gets the credit for the Exodus? Isn't the important thing that the slaves go free? In fact, it matters a great deal. Had Pharaoh let the slaves go when Moses first asked him to, without all those plagues, perhaps because they were no longer as useful economically as they had been years earlier, perhaps because, like his predecessor in Joseph's time, he had a dream about the downtrodden rising up against him, the lesson would have been that the well-being of the oppressed depends on the benevolence of the ruler. The ruler decides whether people will be slaves or free. But because Pharaoh insisted on holding on to his slaves as plague after plague rained down on his country, the moral of the story is that freedom for all is the will of God, even if powerful rulers oppose it.

Compare the biblical story of the Exodus to another account of slaves being freed. One hundred forty years ago, the United States was bitterly divided over the question of slavery. Strange as it may seem today, some justified it on scriptural grounds, others on grounds of economic necessity. Some called for its abolition for economic reasons—the invention of new machinery, the proliferation of small farms instead of large plantations, had made slavery less necessary. Other voices insisted that even if slaveowners benefited from owning slaves, it was morally and religiously wrong for one human being to own another.

Did it make a difference which line of reasoning inspired the abolitionist cause? I believe it did. For one thing, people are more likely to fight and to risk their lives for deeply held ideals than for what is profitable. (God wins over Marx every time.) For another, if slavery was wrong because it was no longer financially advantageous, does that mean it was right when it made financial sense? Would it be right again should financial circumstances change?

The struggle against the enslavement of one human being by another, whether fought in nineteenth-century America or in ancient Egypt, was justified because slavery is wrong. It is wrong in all generations and in all economic circumstances. The freedom and dignity of every person of every race and gender is not a gift dispensed by a benevolent ruler. It is a blessing each of us received from our Creator. That is what the Bible is saying when it declares that the Exodus must be seen as God's doing, not Pharaoh's, "for the sake of God's great name." Freeing the enslaved must be seen as an aspect of what kind of God He is and what kind of world He demands, not what kind of man and king Pharaoh is.

In 1923, the theologian-philosopher Martin Buber wrote an immensely influential little book entitled *I and Thou*. Buber's main point in the book is that there are two ways of relating to other people in our lives: as objects ("How can I use that person?"), or as subjects ("I know what I'm feeling; what is the other person feeling?"). In Buber's terms, there are "I-It" and "I-Thou" relationships. In an I-Thou relationship, we see the other person as a subject, someone who comes to the encounter with needs and feelings of his or her own. In I-It relationships, we see the other person as a means to an end. We are concerned only with our own feelings, not with the feelings of the other person. (I am reminded of the woman in my congregation who to this day has not forgiven me for leaving her son's Bar Mitzvah celebration early when I learned that my wife had been taken to the hospital to give birth to our second child.)

Think of it this way: You are having lunch in a restaurant. The waitress seems distracted, asking you to repeat your order, bringing you regular coffee instead of the decaf you requested. How do you respond? Are you simply annoyed with her, maybe to the extent of not leaving her a tip or complaining to the manager? Or do you get beyond annoyance and wonder what might be bothering her? Has she just come from having a biopsy taken at the doctor's office? Does she have a sick child at home? Is her marriage in trouble? In other words, do you see her as a person or simply as a vehicle for bringing you your lunch, like a vending machine that you are entitled to kick and curse if it doesn't operate properly.

In a memoir, Buber tells the story of how he came to his theory of I-Thou and I-It. Shortly after he had established himself as a professor of philosophy in Germany, a young student came to see him with a personal problem. The student had received his draft notice to serve in the German army in World War One. He was a pacifist by nature and afraid of being killed in battle, but at the same time he was a loyal and fiercely patriotic German. He asked Buber what he should do, serve his country and risk being killed or claim conscientious objector status and perhaps leave another young man to be killed in his place. Buber was in the midst of thinking through a difficult theological-philosophical problem and was annoyed by the young man's claim on his time and attention. He said something along the lines of, That's a serious dilemma; do what you think is right. The young man, in despair for lack of guidance, committed suicide, and Buber, for the rest of his life, felt a measure of guilt for not being more present to that young man, for seeing him only as an interruption and not as a human soul in torment. He felt he had sinned against the image of God in that young student by treating him as an object, not as a subject with needs and feelings.

For Buber, the ultimate sin is to use another person as a means to an end, without regard for the person's feelings. In that light, even the most intimate relationships can be I-It or I-Thou. Teenagers can see a boyfriend or girlfriend as a way of showing off to others how attractive they are, or as a way of assuaging their loneliness. We can want to sleep with someone in order to take advantage of that person, to "score," to validate our masculine or feminine charm, without regard for the damage it might do to the other person's sense of self-worth. Or we can make the relationship a genuine merging of two souls. In the movie *A Touch of Class,* the hero, played by George Segal, is deeply involved in an extramarital affair but reluctant to leave his wife. He shares his dilemma with a friend who asks him two questions: "Do you really love her [the girlfriend]?" "Yes, I do." "Do you really love her enough to let her go because you're being unfair to her?"

As Buber sees it, God relates to every one of us in an I-Thou manner. God never "uses" us to meet His needs. God is always aware of our feelings, seeing us as subjects, never as mere objects. An employer or parent might be upset and angry when someone disobeys his instructions because he sees it as a challenge to his authority. God is upset and angry when His children disobey Him because

He knows that the rules and commands are for our own good.

God has no ego. He cares for us for our sakes, not for His. What then does it mean to say that He leads us in straight paths for His name's (that is, His reputation's) sake, that He brought Israel out of Egypt in a manner that would reflect glory on Him, not on Pharaoh? Why do Christians celebrate and beatify saints who live and die in a manner that testifies to their love of God? Why is the greatest virtue in Judaism the performance of an act, whether returning a lost object or acting heroically in a crisis, that causes people to be impressed that a person's religion could inspire him to act that way? I think the reason is that, when we see the hand of God in the good things that happen to us, we come to see the world differently. We see it more hopefully, we recognize the sacred dimension of history and of our own lives. If we see the freeing of the Israelite slaves or the end of slavery in the United States as the will of God rather than resulting from human kindness or economic trends, then those who are enslaved today can hope for freedom because God is permanent while human generosity is unreliable. When we see the victory of the United States over Hitler, or the Maccabees defeating the mighty Greek army in biblical times, not only as a military outcome but as an instance of God giving victory to the forces of good over the forces of evil, then we can be more optimistic about the ultimate triumph of goodness in the next conflict. If we look at the times in our own lives when events led us in a roundabout path, when disappointment opened a door to fulfillment, and if we recognize the hand of God in those events rather than attributing them to good luck or to our deserving them, then we will be more hopeful and less discouraged by the next disappointment.

God does so many things for us. What can we possibly do for God in return? What gifts can we give Him to show our love and our gratitude? If God has no ego, what can we do to please Him? We can do two things. First, we can give God the benefit of the doubt. It has been said that patience with people is love and patience with God is faith. Faith does not mean believing in God's existence. It means believing in God's reliability, believing that God can be counted on. When my wife says that she doesn't worry about what I do when I'm away from home on a business trip because she believes in me, it's not my existence she is affirming; it's my trustworthiness. When things are going badly, when forces of evil and selfishness seem to have the upper hand, we can give God the gift of not despairing, not giving up on Him. And second, we can make God look good by the way we live our lives so that others will be inspired to follow us and walk in God's ways. There are people whose theologies I do not share, but I consider their religions to be "true" when I see the way they live their faith. When people see that we are charitable, that we refrain from gossip, that we work to make our communities better as an expression of our religious values, we do good things and walk in straight paths "for His name's sake."

To attach the name of God to the sunrise, to the serendipitous discovery of a medical cure, to the resiliency of the human soul in time of trouble is not a case of God's selfishly claiming all the good things for Himself. It is more like a designer or manufacturer putting his brand name on a fine article of clothing or on an appliance. It is a promise of quality and reliability. Life holds many gifts for us—the sun coming out after the storm, friends to pick us up when we have fallen, a door opening in front of us when another one has just slammed shut behind us. When we speculate on the paths our lives have taken and all the good things that have come our way, some of which we could never have anticipated, let us pause to thank God for leading us in roundabout paths, to end up where we were meant to be, for His name's sake.

CHAPTER EIGHT

Though I Walk Through the Valley of the Shadow of Death

In my study at home, I have a shelf filled with books I wrote but cannot read. They are the translations of my books into foreign languages, some of them fairly exotic—Icelandic, Afrikaans, Croatian—and almost all of them inaccessible to me. But when I pick up one of my books translated into a language of which I have at least a modest reading knowledge—Hebrew, German, Spanish—I find my ideas but not my voice. The translator has done an excellent job of finding the equivalent in her language for what I have written in English, but something has gotten lost in the process.

There is an Italian proverb, *traduttore traditore,* which means "to translate is to betray." No matter how well a translation is done, the proverb implies, it will never capture the essential flavor of the original. I have been told by people in a position to know that, were I to read Homer in the original Greek, Dante in Italian, or Pushkin in Russian, it would be a totally different experience than reading them in the best English translation. And I have never read an English version of the Bible, even the majestic King James version that has so enriched our language, that captured the concise power of the original Hebrew.

But every now and then, a translator is touched with inspiration and comes up with the perfect equivalent, or on rare occasions an even better rendering. We have an example of that in this key verse from the Twenty-third Psalm. Most Bible scholars agree that the Hebrew text does not speak of "the shadow of death." In all likelihood, the original Hebrew word was *tzalamut,* deep darkness. The psalmist is saying that, even when he walks in a dark valley, despite the uneasy feeling he and most of us have in the dark, he is not afraid. But the editors of the King James Bible read it as two words, *tzal mavet,* the shadow of death, and in a sense they may have understood what the author was trying to say better than the author himself did. It is not the fact of death, but the knowledge that we will one day die, that casts a shadow over our lives.

Father Leonard Dubi, a Catholic priest interviewed by Studs Terkel for his book *Will the Circle Be Unbroken?,* tells him, "I don't fear death, I fear dying. I fear the kinds of dying I've seen people experience, terribly painful moments, moments when they're alone." Having seen others die, he is haunted by the shadow of death. Would we be better off if we did not know that death awaited us?

The first amoeba that ever existed is still alive, dividing and redividing but never mating and never giving birth to brand-new amoebas. But above a certain level of complexity, all living creatures are mortal. From insects to elephants, we are born, mature, reproduce, and die. Human beings are unique in that we are the only creatures who know throughout our lives that we are fated to die, and that knowledge can cast a shadow over even the sunniest of our days. I think that was what God had in mind when he warned Adam and Eve against eating of the Tree of Knowledge, "for on the day you eat of it, you will die." They did not die that day, but part of the knowledge they gained, the knowledge that would separate them from all other animals, was the knowledge of their mortality.

Young children may not understand the permanence of death. They see Wile E. Coyote being hit by a falling anvil or having a bomb explode as he is holding it, but he keeps on running. They see actors killed in a movie or television program show up again in another movie or summer rerun. They can't understand why a deceased grandparent won't be able to play with them anymore. Adolescents feel they can be extravagant with time, comfortably wasting time, impatient for their next birthday or milestone, because they believe they have an endless supply of tomorrows. It has been said that eighteen-year-old young men make the best soldiers and the worst drivers because they believe they are going to live forever. That may be why the typical response of an adolescent to the death of a young person is as likely to be anger at the unfairness—"it's not supposed to happen this way"—as sadness at the loss.

But all of us, at one age or another, have incorporated the inevitability of death into our thinking about our lives (though when I was a congregational rabbi, I was repeatedly surprised by the number of people who had not bought a cemetery plot or made out a will). What does it mean to live under "the shadow of death," to live with the knowledge that we will die? Are we better off living with the shadow of death, the knowledge that we are mortal, rather than having death take us by surprise?

A gay man in America lives in the shadow of death, never unmindful of the fact that he is one blood test away from being told he has an incurable disease. A teenager growing up in an inner-city neighborhood plagued by guns and drug dealers, too often hearing gunshots and police sirens, feels haunted by the shadow of death. People living in a war zone know the feeling. My father lived through World War One in a Lithuanian town that was fiercely fought over by the Russian and German armies. He remembered people asking one another every morning, "Who died in the bombing last night?" The woman whose mother and sister died of breast cancer, the man who had a first heart attack at age forty-five, know what it is to have the shadow of death loom over even the brightest day.

You may remember from reading the Bible that, when

God made the world, He concluded each day of Creation by contemplating what He had done that day and pronouncing it "good." When the world was finished, God looked at it and declared it "very good." One Jewish sage suggested that the words "very good" included the inescapable fact of death. He read *tov meod,* "very good," as if it were *tov mot,* "death is good." It strikes one as a strange thing to say. Is there a way in which we can say not that death is good, but that the shadow of death, the knowledge that we are mortal, can be seen as a good thing?

Sometimes the anticipation of death can invest our days and our decisions with meaning. A person can respond to the inevitability of death in one of several ways. He can choose the path of self-indulgence, saying to himself, Eat, drink, and be merry for tomorrow I may die. He can respond with despair, thinking, What is the point of doing anything since nothing lasts?, like the author of the biblical book Ecclesiastes, or like Woody Allen's recollection of himself in one of his films as a child who proclaims "What's the point of doing homework?" after learning that the sun is going to disappear and all life will end in six billion years. Or he can choose to say to himself, Since my days are limited, let me make the most of them. Since every choice I make rules out the alternatives and since I won't live long enough to do everything, my choices say something about what I value most. This may be what the psalmist had in mind when he wrote, "Teach us to number our days [that is, to make every day count] that we may gain a heart of wisdom" (Psalm 90:12). In Homer's *The Odyssey,* the gods are envious of Ulysses for being mortal for just that reason. His choices matter more than theirs do because he does not have endless time to go back and do things differently.

The poet Wallace Stevens once wrote, "Death is the mother of beauty." What those words say to me is that we cherish the beauty of a sunrise, of a New England autumn, of a relationship, of a child's hug, precisely because those things will not be around forever and neither will we be around forever to enjoy them.

Philosophers may tell us that death is really a good thing, that living forever would be unbearable, and that knowing we are mortal forces us to concentrate on what we want our lives to be about. But despite their wise words, it is still a scary thing to know that we will one day die and leave behind those we love and those who love us. The valley of the shadow is a frightening, unsettling place, but religion has something to offer us to make it less frightening. If Father Dubi's pastoral (and perhaps personal) experience taught him that the hardest part of contemplating death is the loneliness, the fear that people will leave us as they see us about to leave them, perhaps the antidote for that fear is the faith that we are never alone, not even at the hour of our death. As the psalmist will tell us in the very next line, even in the face of death, perhaps especially in the face of death, God is with us.

Many psychologists writing on the subject of death have emphasized that ultimately every one of us dies alone. They are right in the sense that death happens to us as individuals. Even victims of a plane crash, though they may die simultaneously, experience death individually. But what if we were to understand death not from a psychological viewpoint that is necessarily individualistic, but from a religious viewpoint that can be relational, rooted in the I-Thou relationship that God has with every one of us? For me as a Jew, the Crucifixion does not and cannot have the same theological meaning that it has for a Christian. But nonetheless I am deeply moved by the idea of God sharing in the death of a good person. God does not inflict the death, not as a punishment and not as part of a divine master plan. God shares the pain that occurs when one soul is pulled out of its network of relationships, like a tooth extracted from a person's jaw. God does not die, God does not share the death. But God shares the pain of death to dilute it and make it less painful. When my time comes, I will feel less alone because I will know that God is not only grieving for me but is with me at that moment.

In the Jewish tradition, a mourner is asked to respond to the death of a loved one with the Mourners' Prayer, the Kaddish. Surprisingly, the prayer contains no reference to death, to the deceased, or to the experience of bereavement. It asks that God's name be expanded and sanctified in this world. One explanation of the Kaddish suggests that, when a good person dies, God is somehow diminished. At least in this world, God is slightly less present than He was when that person was alive. It is as if a little bit of God has disappeared with the person's death because God has shared the death experience with that person. So we pray that, through our actions, God's presence be expanded and magnified to fill that vacuum.

There are times when the shadow that death casts over our lives is not the prospect of our own death but the death of people close to us, people we love. They die and the sunshine goes out of our lives. All we can see is the darkness. The pain and grief we feel at a time like that is the price we pay for having loved. If we didn't love people that much, it would not hurt nearly as much when we lose them, whether to death or other circumstances.

To love someone is to make yourself vulnerable. It means taking off the armor you habitually wear to protect yourself against the forces in the world that would hurt you. To love someone is to say to that person, Being close to you is so important to me that I will give you the power to hurt me because I trust you not to use that power. Sometimes people do take advantage of another's vulnerability—spouses and lovers who grow angry at each other, parents who abuse their children physically or verbally, children who find ways to hurt their parents by hurting themselves with drugs or alcohol or by their choice of a career or marriage partner. And of course everyone you love will hurt you, or be hurt by you, when they or you die.

I have known people who had been hurt early in life by someone they loved and responded by being afraid ever to love again. They would use people or they would try to get close to people, but they could never bring themselves to be brave and trusting enough to take off the psychological armor they wore to protect themselves. A. E. Housman has a poem that begins

> When I was one-and-twenty, I heard a wise man say,
> "Give crowns and pounds and guineas but not your
>   heart away. . . ."

The poem concludes, "And I am two-and-twenty and oh, 'tis true, 'tis true." That is, he made the youthful "mistake" I suspect we all recognize, of loving someone and being heartbroken when that love proved unreliable. But think of how much you miss when you are afraid to love, afraid to "give . . . your heart away" because you are afraid of losing the one you love. Think of all the joy you rule out of your life when you try to avoid the shadow of death and loss at all costs. Sigmund Freud was wrong when he said that people choose between pleasure and pain. The real choice is between inviting both pleasure and pain into our lives or else opting for a life of numbness, a life without feeling, so that life will never hurt us.

"The shadow of death." What is a shadow? A shadow is caused when something blocks out the light. There cannot be shadows without the sun shining, and the shadow of death cannot blight our lives unless the experience of death comes between us and the sun. Similarly, the pain we feel at the loss of love is, in its own way, a tribute to how precious and warming that love was to us. I am reminded of the line in Kahlil Gibran's *The Prophet,* when he speaks of those who "stand with their backs to the sun and what is the sun to them but a caster of shadows?"

For all those who hurt because of the loss of love, for all those who in their moments of despair see God and God's world with its inevitable prospect of death as a "caster of shadows," I would call their attention to one word in the line from the Twenty-third Psalm that we are discussing, a word they may not have noticed: "Though I walk *through* the valley of the shadow of death. . . ."

I have known people who were hurt by life and chose to remain in the shadow. They never made it through the valley to a place where the sun could shine on them again. I often wondered why they chose to stay there. After our son's death, my wife and I joined a support group for bereaved parents, The Compassionate Friends. It was a lifeline for us when we needed it, and we remain grateful for its help. We would meet once a month and go around the table, each family recounting the story of their loss of a child. We discovered how important it was to be with people who understood our emotional need to tell the story over and over again when our friends were telling us "get over it and get on with your life," and we discovered how helpful we could be to other bereaved parents by telling them that we had the same fantasies and the same guilt feelings they did.

My wife and I attended for some three or four months and then "graduated," feeling we had gotten what we needed from the group. But there were parents there who had not missed a meeting in ten years. That bothered me. It seemed that being parents of a child who died was such an important part of their identity that they were reluctant to give it up. They remained in the valley of the shadow instead of finding their way through it. I say this not to judge them—twenty-five years after my son's death, it remains the single defining moment of my life—but to try to understand them.

I have met many people over the years, counseling them as their rabbi or hearing their stories after a lecture, who were stuck in the valley of the shadow of death, unable to move out of the shadows. In some cases, their misfortune confirmed their own sense, perhaps born out of an unhappy childhood, that they "deserved" to have such things happen to them, that they had no right to be happy, that they were not worthy of warmth and sunlight.

Sometimes men and women who have never been the center of attention before in their lives find people fussing over them in their bereavement and are reluctant to give that up. By remaining stuck in the valley of the shadow, they believe they continue to have a claim on our sympathy.

I think of two women in my community who were each widowed in their early seventies. Both were in reasonably good health; neither was left with major financial problems. But if their situations were similar, their responses were very different. One spoke of her love for her husband and her lack of resentment at having had to care for him through an extended illness. But then she went on to make a new life for herself. She would meet with friends for lunch. She would travel to places she had never been able to visit when she was caring for a sick husband at home. She would occasionally enjoy the company of gentlemen her own age. The second woman never got over her husband's death. Being a widow became her entire identity. Virtually every sentence she spoke was a lament for having to live alone. She had grown comfortable in the valley of the shadow and had forgotten that it was possible to live anywhere else.

In many animal fables, from Greek mythology to Winnie-the-Pooh, the owl is the symbol of wisdom. But in Jewish lore, the owl is a non-kosher bird, unacceptable in Jewish homes, because it dwells in darkness, shunning the daylight. I have known people like that.

And then there are those who remain in the shadows out of a misplaced sense of love and loyalty. They are afraid that if they ever get over their loss—of a mate, of a child, even of a parent—they will lose that loved one permanently. Death had deprived them of someone's physical presence; permitting themselves to enjoy life, to laugh and bask in the sunshine again, would mean giving up that person's memory. They say to themselves and others, "How can I go out and enjoy myself when she's not around to share it with me? How can I go places and do things we used to do together?" That is why, when I speak to groups of bereaved parents, I tell them that, along with the rest of their child's possessions—his books, his CDs— they have inherited his unlived years, all the things he or she never got to do. Parents honor their child's memory best not by saying "I'll never get over it" but by living those "inherited" years as fully and as meaningfully as possible.

Like many therapists, I have had occasion to ask a grieving spouse or parent, "Had you been the one to die first, what advice would you have left for your loved one? How would you have wanted him to spend the rest of his life?" The answer has almost always been, "I would have wanted him to miss me, but I would have told him to live as fully as possible, as a tribute to the life we shared." I follow that up with the obvious suggestion that they follow that advice themselves.

That is why the Jewish calendar asks us to pause five times a year, on the four holiday seasons and on the anniversary of a death, to remember those whom we have loved and lost. It is a way of giving us permission to go on with our lives without having to fear that we will forget, that we will leave precious but painful memories behind. I urge people to see that the same love that makes the death of a person hurt so much is the love that should inspire us to keep walking through the valley, in tribute to the power and holiness of life even in the face of death.

The author of the Twenty-third Psalm, a man who, in Robert Frost's phrase, had been "acquainted with the night," knew from personal experience what it feels like to find himself in the valley of the shadow. But he also knew that the valley is a temporary lodging, not a permanent home. Human beings are not fashioned to live in darkness. Even as our eyes require light, even as our bodies require sunshine, our souls need companionship, laughter, a sense of purpose. He came to learn that God's role is not to protect us from pain and loss, but to protect us from letting pain and loss define our lives. The psalmist turned to God and God worked a miracle for him. The miracle was not that his loved one came back to life. The miracle was that he found his way out of the valley of the shadow. And that *is* a miracle. The valley of the shadow of death can be a seductive place, impossible to enjoy but hard to leave.

This is the advice the psalmist would give us: Don't be afraid to love people, to "give your heart away," though love inevitably brings pain. Don't be afraid of the pain of losing, whether it is the prospect of your own death or the death of someone you love. Trust God to enter into your pain and make it less painful, less frightening. Move on, taking one step and then another, no matter how dark the valley in which you find yourself. There has never been a tunnel so long that it did not ultimately emerge into daylight or a night so dark that it did not ultimately yield to the dawn.

Think of all the people you know, all the people you have read about or seen on television, to whom terrible things happened—betrayal, bereavement, crippling injuries—and somehow they found the strength to go on. They found a sense of purpose to their lives, refusing to let the tragedy define them. (To define, the dictionary reminds us, means to limit, to set boundaries.) Let God take you by the hand as He did for them and lead you through the valley of darkness.

CHAPTER NINE

I Will Fear No Evil
for Thou Art with Me

With this verse, we reach the heart of the psalm, the words and the ideas that touch our souls and move us to cherish these lines. Everything until now has led up to these words; everything that follows will draw upon them. Now we can discover the essence of the psalm's appeal. Martin Buber once tried to explain the difference between theology and religion by saying that theology was *talking about* God while religion was *experiencing* God. The difference between them, he suggested, was the difference between reading a menu and eating dinner. Theology can be enlightening. It can help us understand. It can instruct our minds. But only actual contact with God can nourish our souls.

Bearing that distinction in mind, let us look again at the words of the Twenty-third Psalm. When is the psalmist offering us theology, talking to us *about* God? And when is he offering religion, the experience of *encountering* God?

When does the psalmist refer to God as "He" and when as "Thou"?

> The Lord is my shepherd; I shall not want.
> *He* makes me to lie down in green pastures.
> *He* leads me beside the still waters.
> *He* restores my soul.
> *He* guides me in straight paths for *His* name's sake.
> Yea, though I walk through the valley of the shadow
>   of death,
> I will fear no evil for *Thou* art with me. (italics added)

The conventional assumption is that when bad things happen to us, they cause us to lose faith in God. "How can there be a God in a world where children die?" "Why do I have to go through this? I don't deserve it." And all too often, that conventional wisdom is true. When my wife and I attended monthly meetings of The Compassionate Friends after our son's death, we would meet people who were so angry at God that they had not set foot in a church or synagogue for years. They had missed family weddings and holiday celebrations rather than find themselves in the company of people praising God. There were times when I would not tell the other parents I was a rabbi, so as not to provoke the pain and rage that religion stirred up in those people.

But just as often, perhaps more often, I have seen things work the other way. People for whom the existence of

God was a remote, abstract, theological concept, people who believed in the existence of God the way they believed in the existence of Mongolia ("I've never been there, but people tell me there is such a place and I'm not inclined to take issue with them"), suddenly find themselves in the valley of the shadow, and what had been abstract and remote suddenly becomes pulsatingly real. At that point, they find themselves saying, "God, I never could have made it through the valley and into the sunlight without Your help and support, without the people You inspired to reach out to me, without the courage and resiliency You planted in me."

Note that the psalmist does not say that he will fear no evil because there is no such thing as evil, because everything is part of God's plan and ultimately works out for the best. Nor does he say that he will fear no evil because he is a good person and evil befalls only people who deserve it. He says that there is evil in the world and that he is as vulnerable to it as anyone else, but that doesn't frighten him because God is real and God is on his side.

God's promise was never that life would be fair, that if you were a good person, illness and injury would spare you and would happen only to people who deserved it. A teacher of mine used to warn us that expecting the world to treat you fairly because you were a good person was like expecting the bull not to charge you because you were a vegetarian. God's promise was that when we had to face the pain and unfairness of the world as we inevitably would, we would not have to face it alone, for He would be with us.

Why should that help? Why should it be easier to face life's problems with support than to face them by ourselves? One reason, as I mentioned earlier, is our almost irresistible tendency to ask, "What did I do to deserve this?" There seems to be a corner of our minds that insists on making sense of the world (even when the world doesn't make sense, as it often doesn't). We are so much more comfortable in a world of cause and effect, a world in which there is a reason for everything, than we are in a world where things "just happen." And sometimes that causes us to blame ourselves for our misfortune rather than to blame bad luck. Why did a careless driver speaking on a cell phone crash into my parked car? Because the other day I was reading the new car ads and wishing my car were in worse shape so that I could trade it in for a newer model. Why did I come down with the flu? Just the other day I scolded my sister for getting sick because she wasn't taking care of herself, and this is God teaching me a lesson.

Elaine Pagels, in her book *Adam, Eve, and the Serpent,* explains our tendency to blame ourselves for the bad things that happen to us by writing, "many people would rather feel guilty than feel powerless." The teenage boy whose father dies of cancer and who is convinced that his angry thoughts about his father caused the death, is saying two things that resonate in his adolescent soul. He is saying, *I am a wicked person; I made my father die. People should shun and condemn me.* And he is saying, *I am an immensely powerful person. I am the master of life and death. I decide who shall live and who shall die. People had better take me seriously.*

When something bad happens to us, it is a short step from assuming we did something to cause it to believing that we are guilty of deserving our fate and now that our guilt is known (he must have done something terrible; why else would this have happened to him?), everybody will know the truth about us and will reject us. That is why it is so helpful, so healing, when people gather around us in our pain and grief, not answering our questions about God or explaining our misfortune, but just holding our hands, drying our tears, writing letters of condolence, telling us, in words and gestures, "You're a good person; you don't deserve this."

In the wake of the bombing of the Murrah Federal Building in Oklahoma City in 1995, I was invited to go to Oklahoma City to conduct a workshop for clergy and social workers on how to help the victims' families. Afterward I met with the bereaved families at the governor's mansion. I asked each of them, "In the six weeks since the bombing, what one thing more than anything else helped you find the strength to go on, to wake up every morning and face the world, with that gaping hole in the world where your loved one had been?" Every single family member gave me the same answer: people. Friends, neighbors, even total strangers coming up to them and telling them how bad they felt for them, for what they had to go through. The cure for feeling that you are a bad person and you deserve what happened is to have someone, or many someones, tell you, "You're a good person and I feel bad for you."

I made that point in a lecture one evening, and afterward a woman came up to me to share her story. She told me how she was on her way out of the office for a coffee break when she saw a coworker whom she knew casually sitting and looking out of the window. She said to her, "I'm going for coffee. Would you like to come along?" The woman thought for a moment and said, "Sure." Over coffee, the coworker said, "I have to tell you what your invitation meant to me. Two days ago, my longtime boyfriend left me, telling me on the way out all the things that were wrong with me. I was devastated. I was sure no one would ever love me again. When you saw me staring out the window a few minutes ago, I was trying to summon up the courage, or maybe it wouldn't be courage, to open it and jump out, taking my life because I felt so alone. Your invitation to join you for coffee called me back to life. It said to me that there were still people in the world who cared about me. I don't know how to thank you."

Some years ago, a professor of psychology at a major university conducted an experiment in pain tolerance. He invited several dozen students to measure how long they could keep a bare foot immersed in a bucket of ice water.

One of the things he learned was that if there was someone else in the room, a person could keep his foot in the bucket nearly twice as long. The presence of another caring person doubles the amount of pain someone can endure. Guilt feels less deserved, pain is less painful, misfortune is less oppressive, when someone is there with you.

The lesson for all of us is: When we know people who have encountered misfortune, the best thing we can do for them is simply to be with them. We don't need to explain their suffering or try to make them feel better by telling them of people who are worse off. We certainly don't need to defend God; God can take care of Himself. At a time like that, people crave consolation more than explanation. Simply being there, silently holding someone's hand, is what helps most. And if you are the afflicted one, the best thing you can do at a time like that is to shun the temptation to close yourself off in a dark room with the shades drawn and feel sorry for yourself. At a time like that, you need to let people into your life. Even if sometimes those people say the wrong things, even if in their discomfort and clumsiness they say hurtful things, you need to listen to the intention behind the words and hear the unarticulated message that they care for you and want to ease your pain by sharing it.

It is easier to face a troubling present and an uncertain future when you don't have to face it alone. But helpful as it is to have someone with you, it is even more helpful when that someone is God. When my wife and I learned that our three-year-old son had the incurable condition that would cause his premature death, I was wounded not only by the prospect of losing him but by the sense that God was doing this to me. Like most of us, I was raised to believe in an all-powerful God who controlled everything that happened in the world, and if we could not understand God's ways, the limitation was ours, not God's. Up until that day, I thought I had a deal with God. I would be a good, religiously observant person. I would work night and day to persuade others to be good and religiously observant. And partly as a reward, partly as an inducement to those others, God would bless and protect my family. When I absorbed the shattering news the doctors had for us, I couldn't help feeling that I had held up my end of the bargain but God had just defaulted on His. It became desperately important for me to know whether God was on my side or on the side of the illness. Only when I came to believe that God did not control genetics or laws of nature, that fire burns and bullets harm good people and bad people alike, that God may have cared about what kind of people my wife, my son, and I were, but nature was blind, was I able to turn to religion to sustain me in my despair.

When the psalmist writes, "I will fear no evil for Thou art with me," he is not only saying, I can handle this because I am not alone. He is saying, I can handle this because God is with *me* and not on the side of the illness or accident. I can handle this because God is on my side and not on the side of the selfish, deceptive people who are embittering my life.

In a seminally important passage in the Bible (Exodus 3:6–14), God appears to Moses at the Burning Bush and directs him to go to Pharaoh and demand that Pharaoh free the Hebrew slaves. Moses responds by asking God, "What is Your name? When I go to Pharaoh and to the Israelites and tell them that You sent me, and they ask me who You are, what am I to say?" At first glance, it sounds like a strange question. (God: Moses, I am the God of your fathers. I want you to change the course of human history by going to Pharaoh and demanding that he set his slaves free. Moses: Excuse me, what was Your name again?) We need to realize that in biblical times, your name was more than your identification. It was your essence; it defined what you were about and what you stood for. Moses was asking God, What kind of god are you? There are fertility gods, gods of war, gods of the harvest. What kind of god are you? God answers him in three words that defy translation, *Ehyeh asher ehyeh*, usually rendered, "I am what I am" or "I will be what I will be." Theologians, who assume that when God speaks, He speaks theology, explain those words to mean "I am pure being." Others understand God to be saying, "What I am is more than you can comprehend." But I have always been drawn to the interpretation that connects God's answer to His use of the word *"Ehyeh"* two verses earlier, when He tells Moses, "When you go to Pharaoh, *I will be with you*" (italics added). For me, that is God's name, the essence of what He is about. God is the one who is with us when we have to do something hard. He is the one who is with us when we are tempted to feel that the world has abandoned us. He is the one who is with us when we feel alone in the valley of the shadow.

Is the conviction that God is on our side really enough to dispel fear? I believe it is, even as a little bit of light is enough to dispel our fear in a room full of darkness. Picture this scene: A child wakes up in the middle of the night in a totally dark bedroom. He is frightened by the noises he hears outside, by the creaking of the walls of his house, the rattling of the windows. But if there is a tiny light in his room, just enough to make the darkness less than total, he is no longer afraid. If he cries out and his mother or father reassures him, "It's all right, we are here, there is nothing to be afraid of," that can dispel his fear.

In the same way, when we find ourselves mired in emotional darkness, when events and people conspire to fill our lives with anguish, it takes only a little ray of light to make the darkness bearable. My teacher Abraham Joshua Heschel once wrote, "Dark for me is the world if not for the knowledge that God listens when I cry." He does not expect God to change things, to eliminate evil, to make his problems disappear. It is enough for him to believe that God is there for him. Then he knows he is not alone. He knows he has not been abandoned.

Now perhaps we can understand why this psalm, more than any other, speaks to our hearts as it does. The words "I will fear no evil for Thou art with me" are the Bible's clearest and most succinct response to the question of why bad things happen to good people. God does not explain; God comforts.

There is a passage in the Book of Exodus (15:22–25) in which the Israelites, thirsty after marching through the Sinai wilderness, come to a pool of brackish water not fit to drink. God shows Moses a tree that, when thrown into the water, sweetens it and makes it drinkable. A commentator imagines an exchange in which Moses asks God, "What was the point of Your creating something utterly useless like undrinkable water? What exactly did You have in mind when You created cockroaches, gypsy moths, scorpions?" God answers, "Moses, this is not a time for theology, for speculating on why certain things exist, for asking God 'Why?' This is a time for action, for doing something to sweeten the bitterness and ease the people's thirst, rather than debate the theological issue of why they are thirsty. You don't have to understand the world and everything in it to make it a better place."

So too the psalmist is saying to us, When bad things happen to you, the challenge is not to explain them, to justify them, or even to accept them. The challenge is to survive them and go on living. And the key to surviving misfortune is the realization that, when bad things happen, God is on our side. The illness, the accident are not God's will. When we choose to affirm life in the face of loss, to affirm goodness in the face of evil, we are on God's side. He is with us and we are with Him, and the future does not frighten us.

CHAPTER TEN

Thy Rod and Thy Staff, They Comfort Me

I had just completed the graveside funeral service for the elderly mother of a congregant when a man came up to me, identified himself as a friend of the man whose mother had died, and said, "When I listened to you recite the Twenty-third Psalm at the graveside, I finally understood one line of it that I had never understood before. It's the one about 'Thy rod and Thy staff, they comfort me.' I never knew what that meant before, but now I think I get it.

"I'm a businessman," he went on. "If I have a problem with one of my suppliers, I call the president of the company to straighten things out. But I usually don't get to talk to the president of the company. I usually end up speaking to a member of his staff who tries to make me feel better. I think that's what the psalm is saying. When people on earth have problems and they call out to God,

God doesn't intervene Himself. He sends a member of His staff to do the comforting. I see you as part of God's team, sent to comfort people and make them feel better when they are hurting."

That was flattering, but of course not what the psalmist had in mind when he wrote that line. The author of the psalm and his audience, knowing more about how shepherds managed their flocks than we do today, understood "staff" to have quite a different meaning. They knew the shepherd used his staff not only to lean on as he walked, but to help straying or fallen sheep climb out of the pits they may have stumbled into. And they knew he used his rod to discipline stubborn sheep that got out of line and wandered into danger. The staff was a symbol of help and support, the rod a symbol of discipline and punishment.

The image of God striking people with His rod, using it to punish even those whom He loves, is common in the Bible. God's word to the prophet Isaiah (10:5) warns Israel that "I will send Assyria, the rod of My anger, against an ungodly people." The author of Lamentations, a survivor of the destruction of Jerusalem in the year 586 B.C.E., writes, "I am the man who has known affliction under the rod of God's wrath" (Lamentations 3:1). Job, suffering and unable to understand why, cries out, "If only He would take His rod away from me" (Job 9:34). God promises the aging King David that He will bless his son Solomon with His favor but will demand righteous behavior from him: "I will be a father to him. When he does wrong, I will chastise him with the rod" (II Samuel 7:14). And perhaps the most familiar reference to the use of the rod to discipline even those whom we love is found in the Book of Proverbs (13:24), "He who spares the rod hates his son."

When the psalmist writes that he is comforted by God's rod and God's staff, he is saying, Two things reassure me that God is in control of the world and the world is not spiraling down into chaos: When I see God sustaining the fallen, giving strength to the abandoned and hope to the desperate, and when I see God making sure that people who have done wrong suffer the consequences of their behavior. He is saying, I need to know that there is compassion in the world, that people who stumble and fall will be helped to their feet. But I also need to know that there is justice in the world, that ultimately people don't get away with evil acts and that sooner or later you pay for every time you do something wrong in life in one currency or another. And I need to know that wrongdoing brings down punishment on good people who slip even as it does on thoroughly wicked people ("When he does wrong, I will chastise him with the rod"), because otherwise how can I be sure that good people won't be tempted into occasional misbehavior? I need to know that our God is a God of forgiveness, a God of second chances who picks us up and wipes us off when we have fallen and soiled ourselves. But I also need to know that God takes my behavior seriously and holds me accountable for what I do, because if He doesn't, why should I?

We can certainly agree that it would be comforting to believe that God sustains the innocent (even when He can't completely protect them from misfortune) and that He arranges for wrongdoers to suffer the consequences of their misbehavior. It offends us when people seem to be getting away with doing wrong. I have lost count of the number of people who have urged me to write a book called *When Good Things Happen to Bad People* because the prosperity of the wicked bothers them as much as the suffering of the righteous does. But does the rod of God really come down hard on wrongdoers? Are the laws of morality built into the universe as firmly as the laws of gravity and chemical reactions, so that people who lie and steal will be punished as predictably as people who overeat will gain weight?

I don't need to believe that God *punishes* us, that He actively intervenes to chastise wrongdoers, like the mother in the playground who tells her child, "You see, God made you fall down when you ran away after I told you not to run." It is enough for me to believe in *consequences* rather than punishments. Wrong behavior carries with it the seeds of its own retribution. Smokers get lung cancer, drunk drivers cause accidents, and philanderers never know the satisfaction of real love, not because God's wrath is called down on them but because their actions have defied the order of God's world.

For many years, I wanted to believe that what the psalmist believes, both here and in the Ninety-second Psalm ("the wicked may spring up as the grass . . . only to be destroyed forever" [Psalm 92:8]), was, in fact, the way the world worked. And a few years ago, I was given reason to believe that it was indeed true.

Researchers at Duke University Medical Center in North Carolina set out to test whether Type-A personalities, the intense, driven, achievement-obsessed people who often rise to the top of organizations because they never waste a moment and are always looking for an edge, would end up making themselves sick. Would they drive themselves to high blood pressure, heart attacks, and ulcers as the price of their success? The researchers assembled several hundred unmistakable Type A's and ran them through a battery of medical examinations. The result: Some of their subjects did indeed show signs of cardiovascular problems, but most were fine. In fact, many were healthier than the average man their age. And this seems to have been the key: A man who is a Type A because he enjoys a challenge, because he finds it deeply satisfying that a project went well as a result of his being in charge, because he likes to look out from his office and see a company or a department running better than it did before he took over, will probably be fine. But a man who is a Type A because he believes that it's a jungle out there, that you can't trust anyone, that you've always got to be looking out for the guy who's trying to cheat you; the man whose definition of success is looking out for number one, putting one over on the other person before he can put one over on you, is likely to make himself sick.

To me, the most important lesson of the Duke study is that human beings are not meant to be hostile, suspicious, or envious of one another. Just as our bodies are designed so that certain ways of living promote health and others—too much eating and drinking, smoking, not getting enough sleep—harm us physically, I believe that our souls are fashioned so that certain kinds of behavior nourish the soul and other kinds are toxic to body and soul alike. Human beings were made by God to be honest and helpful. When we act that way we feel better, as we have all learned when we have gone out of our way to do someone a favor. When we deny our humanity by lying, cheating, or acting selfishly, we feel estranged from our true selves, even as we feel in the aftermath of overeating or excessive drinking. Live right and you will be sustained by God's staff; live wrong and you will feel the impact of God's rod.

When I was growing up in the 1940s, lots of people smoked without worrying that they were damaging their health. Doctors appeared in cigarette ads to endorse one brand or another. Only years later did we learn that smoking could take years off a person's life. What if it turned out that lying was like smoking, that every time we betrayed our soul by telling a lie, we were damaging our health? What if we were to learn that every mean thing we did affected our blood pressure or clogged our arteries, increasing our risk of a heart attack?

Reading *Master of the Senate,* the third volume of Robert Caro's biography of Lyndon Johnson, perhaps the quintessential Type-A personality of our time, I was struck by the fact that Johnson suffered from stress-related illness not when he was working hard but when he was working deceitfully, telling one person one thing and telling another the opposite so that both would think he was on their side.

(This message is not meant to be read backward. I believe that people who violate their human nature make themselves sick. I do not believe that whenever a person gets sick, it is because he or she has done something wrong, somehow "inviting the illness into his life." Sometimes one's only "sin" was sitting too close to someone who had a cold.)

Is it morally acceptable to take pleasure in the tribulations of the wicked, as the psalmist seems to be doing? Do we diminish ourselves morally by feeling happy at another's misfortune, however well deserved? The same Bible that celebrates God's bringing a full measure of judgment on the wicked and blesses those who will kill Babylonian children as the Babylonians killed Israelite children (Psalm 137:9) also instructs us not to rejoice in the downfall of our enemies (Proverbs 24:17).

I have written extensively on the dangers of revenge.

I believe that religion can and must teach us to control our instincts, and I personally have had occasion to rely on God's forgiveness and the forgiveness of others. But I believe it is a mistake for religion to ask us to repress or deny those feelings of wanting to see someone suffer who deserves to suffer, or to feel guilty for having those feelings. In a key candidates' debate during the 1988 presidential election, moderator Bernard Shaw asked George Bush and Michael Dukakis how each of them would respond if his wife were raped and murdered. Dukakis answered with an unemotional, intellectual discourse on the pros and cons of capital punishment. That moment alone may not have cost him the election, but it didn't help his cause. It confirmed people's suspicions of him as an unfeeling technocrat.

Shortly after the election, I was having lunch with a wise friend whose opinion I respect. He had been a Dukakis adviser, and we spoke of the Shaw question and the candidate's answer. My friend observed, "You know, of course, it was the right answer. Crimes like that should be handled by the police and the courts, not by the angry relatives of the victim." It may have been the right answer socially and philosophically, but it was the wrong answer for a presidential candidate trying to get people to identify with him. (Four years later, President Bush lost to Bill Clinton, who did a better job of persuading voters that he felt their "pain.")

It was a great step forward in the history of civilization

when the right to punish was taken away from the victim and his family and given to the authorities. But that change in no way diminishes the irresistible human tendency to feel satisfaction when wrongdoers are punished.

Nor should it. When a crime is committed, when innocent people are hurt or cheated, we instinctively feel, in Hamlet's phrase, "The time is out of joint." The scales of justice are out of balance and need to be set right. There is a tear in the fabric of the universe when a crime remains unsolved, when a criminal evades justice, when a clever lawyer or a bad law permits people to get away with wrongdoing. Only the rod of God falling on the offender restores our faith in the integrity of the world. Is it wrong to wish for bad people to suffer the consequences of their bad behavior? I think it would be wrong not to.

We are left with another, more subtle question: If we find it easier to have faith in God's world when we see God's rod descend on bad people, should it be equally comforting for us to see it fall on basically good people who do bad things—the careful driver who is guilty of a moment's carelessness, the caring parent who responds badly to a child out of fatigue or distraction? The psalmist says that he is comforted by the thought that no one really gets away with anything. Would our world be a better place, a more godly place, if God's laws of retributive consequence cut some slack for nice people?

In a way, they already do. A young mother cornered me after a lecture one evening and told me how guilty she felt every time she yelled at her children because she was in a bad mood. I assured her that if her children understood that she loved them, they would survive her occasional lapses of good judgment. And courts will take a guilty person's overall record into account in passing sentence. But would we want a world with two sets of moral laws, one for people who are usually good and another for people who are usually bad?

I remember a public service announcement some years ago that urged motorists to lock their cars when they parked them and never to leave their keys in an unoccupied car. Locking your vehicle, it said, would not deter the professional car thief. Given enough time, he will find a way to steal it. But it will avoid tempting young people with "crimes of opportunity." A bored teenager with no plans to steal a car might not be able to resist the temptation to take one for a joyride if he saw it sitting there with the keys in it. The more he thinks he can get away with it, the more likely he is to try. Department stores have begun to crack down on teenage shoplifters, threatening them with criminal records rather than parental scolding, not because they are out to ruin a young person's life but because they want to eliminate the mind-set, Let's try it; what's the worst that can happen?

In much the same way, I am writing these lines on an afternoon in mid-April. Forty-eight hours ago, I sent my income tax payment to the Internal Revenue Service. I pay my taxes honestly because I like to think of myself as a law-abiding person and because I appreciate what the government does to make my life and my world better. But I also pay my taxes honestly because I assume that most of my neighbors are paying their taxes honestly and the government is committed to identifying and punishing people who don't. If I ever came to suspect that most people cheat on their taxes, as is the case in some countries, if I ever came to suspect that the government was not equipped or motivated to check on us and that I was being a fool for paying mine, I would like to think that I would continue to obey the law, that I would be uncomfortable enhancing my income by stealing from my country. But the temptation would be there. Nobody likes to be taken advantage of. Like the author of the Twenty-third Psalm, I need to believe in the rod as well as the staff to keep me on the straight path.

It is hard to feel grateful when a patrol car pulls you over and a policeman tickets you for exceeding the speed limit, but it is a mind-set you would do well to cultivate. I am almost inclined to offer this as the hallmark of the truly religious person: not just that you feel guilty when you have been caught doing something wrong, but that you feel reassured that communal standards of behavior are being enforced even if it is at your expense. After all, we and our families drive on those streets, and we will all be safer if the authorities keep them free of speeders and traffic-light violators. When we were children and our parents caught us doing something wrong and disciplined us, we didn't enjoy being punished, but there was something reassuring in finding out that someone was making sure that everybody played by the rules. Because we were basically good people, we understood, however vaguely, that, in the long run, the authority would help us more than it would hurt us.

Good people stumble and fall, but God the faithful shepherd is there to help them recover. Bad people, and some good people who give in to temptation, take things that don't belong to them and hurt others with their thoughtlessness, but sooner or later the bill comes due. The clever liar discovers that no one believes him. The adulterer learns that by choosing casual sex, he has lost out on true love. The violent criminal, even if he avoids prison, comes to live in constant fear of others as violent as he is.

A few years ago, CEOs of start-up companies were taking home tens of millions of dollars a year in salary and bonuses and were everyone's heroes, appearing on television and on magazine covers. Today we have learned that many of those companies were built on a foundation of fraudulent bookkeeping. Yesterday's heroes have been disgraced. The fancy second homes are gone, and some of those CEOs are facing time in prison. I take no personal pleasure in their downfall, but it gives me reason to hope that society will learn from this experience to choose worthier role models, celebrating those who work with the poor and the homeless rather than those who consort only with their fellow multimillionaires.

All around me, I see evidence of God's staff sustaining the fallen and God's rod striking those who call it down upon themselves. And like the psalmist, I am comforted.

CHAPTER ELEVEN

Thou Preparest a Table Before Me in the Presence of Mine Enemies

How did this line find its way into the psalm? After the first two-thirds of the psalm have been filled with images of comfort, gratitude, and trust, themes that will continue for the balance of the psalm, there is something abrupt and unsettling about this line that seems at first glance to reek of spite and taking pleasure in the discomfiture of others. The psalmist seems to be saying, Not only does God supply me with a lavish banquet; what makes it even more pleasurable is that all those people who don't like me will see how God treats me and realize that I am God's favorite. It is the attitude of the man anticipating his high-school reunion and saying to himself, Wait until those guys who made fun of me and those girls who wouldn't go out with me see me drive up in my Mercedes. Three times in the past year, when a colleague asked me what I was working on and I told him I was writing a book about the Twenty-third Psalm, the response in each case was, "What are you doing with the line about preparing a table in the presence of enemies?" It seems to fall short of the lofty spiritual tone of the rest of the psalm. Taking pleasure in the discomfort of others may be a very common human tendency, but is it one that a biblical psalm should celebrate?

At one level, the feelings expressed here may be nothing more than an extension of the previous line: I am comforted when I see good people rewarded (especially when I am one of them) and when I see bad people get their comeuppance (especially when they are people I'm quarreling with). While I realize that life is often unfair and good people can't be protected from misfortune, it reinforces my faith in God's justice when bad people have to swallow the bitter medicine of seeing fortune smile on me. Maybe when bad people are made to witness the good fortune of their more righteous neighbors, they will be moved to change their ways.

But still the aroma of meanspiritedness remains. We would like to think that the experience of God's goodness would cleanse the psalmist's soul of vindictiveness. Theologian and mystic Zalman Schachter, one of a select group of Jewish thinkers who were invited to meet with the Dalai Lama in India some years ago, offers an intriguing interpretation. In a bold and beautiful act of midrash, the Jewish technique of finding ideas in a text that the author didn't know he was putting in there (it has been

suggested that the text represents what the client tells
the therapist and midrash represents what the therapist
hears), Schachter describes how, once a year, he convenes
an imaginary dinner party in his mind, to which he invites
everyone with whom he has had a run-in during the past
year. Everyone with whom he is on bad terms, everyone
who has been mean to him or his family, everyone who
has hurt, offended, or disappointed him is invited to this
imaginary feast. In the course of this mental banquet,
Schachter goes around the table and explains to his guests
that he has invited them to thank them for the various
gifts they have given him during the past year, the lessons
they have taught him. Some have taught him that it is
unrealistic to expect too much from the average person.
Most people will inevitably be more involved with their
own problems than with ours or someone else's. They will
be so distracted by their own issues that they will not hear
our cry for help. As a result, Schachter imagines himself
telling them, he has become more realistic about what he
can expect from people and more aware of the danger of
he himself not hearing the cries of those who turn to him.
He has come to anticipate certain levels of apathy and
selfishness and is now pleasantly surprised by generosity,
instead of anticipating helpfulness and being disappointed
by self-concern. He is learning to phrase his requests of
others in terms of how it will help them rather than in the
abstract rightness of the response.

Others at his imaginary dinner table are there because they have disappointed him by their hypocrisy, by not living up to the standards they claim to believe in. They have taught him a lesson he realizes he might have learned from his own behavior, had he looked at himself as squarely as he looks at others. It is a lot easier to affirm one's belief in a principle than actually to live by it. Sometimes people who say one thing and do another are hypocrites, preaching honesty in business and fidelity in marriage while doing the opposite. But sometimes they are only human. They genuinely believe in supporting charity, but there are so many competing claims for every dollar they earn. They genuinely believe that their lives would be enriched if they attended religious services more often, but the demands on their time are as many as the demands on their purse. They genuinely believe in the importance of their families, but they are so often too tired and too easily upset with the people closest to them that they find it hard to act on their beliefs. We don't accomplish anything by dismissing them as hypocrites. That is all too likely to make them solve the problem by lowering their beliefs to the level of their behavior rather than elevating their behavior. A colleague of mine tells of giving a sermon once pointing out the inconsistency of people who come to synagogue on special occasions but don't come to the weekly Sabbath service. He called it the most effective sermon he ever gave. People listened to him and stopped coming on special occasions. I suspect we would be better off recognizing the legitimacy of what people claim to believe and encouraging them gradually to close the gap between belief and behavior by adjusting their behavior.

Schachter continues around the table at his imaginary banquet, thanking some of his guests for having helped him to understand himself a little better. When something they did upset him deeply, to the point of undermining his relationship with a person, he learned to stop and ask himself, Why was this such a "hot button" for me? Why did I react so strongly and let it upset me? It never occurred to the other person that he or she was doing something monstrous; why did it seem so terrible to me? As a result, he says, he has looked deep into his own soul, traveled back to his childhood in an effort to understand what there was in him that made him react so strongly. Did a slip of the tongue reawaken feelings of his parents favoring an older or younger sibling? Did someone's forgetting a birthday or an appointment stir up feelings of not being taken seriously by people whose love he craved? In the process, he has learned a lot about himself and has learned to put those perceived slights into perspective. He hopes he has made himself less vulnerable to being so easily upset in the future, and for that he is grateful.

Kahlil Gibran, in his meditation *Sand and Foam,* writes, "I have learned silence from the talkative, toleration from the intolerant, and kindness from the unkind. Yet, strange,

I am ungrateful for those teachings." Might we see ourselves learning how to be grateful from Gibran's alleged ingratitude?

I don't believe that Schachter's imaginary dinner was what the psalmist had in mind when he wrote of his enemies witnessing him at the banquet table. But perhaps, like the phrase "the shadow of death," we can see Schachter's interpretation as a "creative misreading," an insight that is true in its own right even as it "misunderstands" the original intent of the line. When we find ourselves in conflict with another person, there may be alternative ways of reframing the conflict. We don't have to ask ourselves, Was it my fault? Did I do something to cause this? And instead of asking, What's wrong with that person that he or she would do such a thing to me? or What's wrong with me that someone would treat me so badly?, we might learn to ask, What can I learn from this incident to reduce the number of people in my life whom I think of as enemies? Sometimes the answer will involve coming to terms with what people are like. People make promises they fully intend to keep, but things come up. It is part of the job of a salesperson (and, as I have learned, of a reporter) to pretend friendship in order to win you over, and we should not feel betrayed or mistreated when a pleasant commercial encounter does not lead to an ongoing relationship.

Sometimes the answer will help you understand yourself better. If an acquaintance criticizes your appearance or what you are wearing and you are upset for the rest of the day, you can ask yourself why that comment bothers you so much. If you think the acquaintance is incorrect, why can't you just shrug it off, telling yourself it reveals more about the other person than it does about you? And if you suspect she may be correct and that is why it bothers you, it may be tactless of her to point it out but perhaps she meant it to be helpful. If you are seething with rage at a classmate who is mean to one of your children, if you are tempted to scold that child or call his parents, or even threaten to hurt the offending child, you should probably stop and ask yourself if you are doing that because you are not sure of your child's ability to take care of himself. And would you be doing your child a greater favor if you supported him emotionally but expressed confidence in his ability to handle the situation on his own?

When I first became a nationally known author in 1981, with the publication of *When Bad Things Happen to Good People,* I began to receive letters by the carload from readers. Ninety-five percent of them were complimentary, and I was deeply gratified by them. A few were efforts to convert me to the faith of the letter writer. And one or two a week would be critical, accusing me of blasphemy and of undermining people's faith. To my distress, I found that one nasty letter bothered me more than fifty nice ones pleased me. I would brood about it for days. If some obscure newspaper ran a negative review of my book, I would be tempted to write an angry letter in response, refuting the criticism point by point. I didn't enjoy feeling that way, and, on an intellectual level, I knew it was foolish of me to let one critical letter bother me that much, but the feelings continued. Finally I realized that instead of asking myself, What's the matter with those people that they don't appreciate me?, I would be better off asking, Why am I so bothered by their criticism? I came to understand that I had not really gotten used to my new status as a best-selling author. I had not anticipated it, and I was having trouble believing it even as it was happening. Every letter that criticized my book upset me precisely because there was a part of me that feared the criticism might be valid. Only when I realized that the source of the problem was within me, not with my critics, and that therefore I had power over my feelings in a way that I had no power over my critics, was I able to overcome those feelings. Had I had the benefit of Zalman Schachter's advice at that time, I would have invited my critics, orthodox Jews, evangelical Christians, and others, to an imaginary dinner (with kosher food for the orthodox guests, of course) and thanked them for prodding me to get over my fears and believe in myself. I would have assured them that they were not, and never should have been, my enemies.

Let me suggest one more way of understanding the troubling line that is the subject of this chapter. The Hebrew word translated "in the presence of [mine enemies]" is *neged,* which ordinarily means "opposite." Might we take the verse to mean, God, You prepare a table before me *in contrast to the people around me,* to whom I turned for emotional nourishment, only to be disappointed.

Many religious traditions understand that when people have been emotionally wounded, bereaved, betrayed, or rejected, they feel empty inside. They guide their followers to respond to their afflicted neighbor with comforting visits and with food. Years ago, when I lost out on a job I really wanted, a good friend instinctively knew what I needed and took my wife and me out for a good dinner. Food as an expression of love and nurturance is a gesture so basic that even infants and family pets understand it. Church members fondly recall the "casserole brigades" that nourished them nutritionally and emotionally in the wake of a loss. There is a beautiful custom in Judaism know as the "meal of replenishment." Mourners return from the cemetery to find that friends have prepared a meal for them, filling the emptiness in their hearts not only with bagels and coffee, but with a statement of caring.

Could the psalmist be saying, When something bad happened to me, I turned to my friends for support, for the reassurance that I was not a bad person, that I did not deserve this fate? Some were wonderful, caring, supportive friends. But some people on whom I counted turned out to be false friends. They were not, or maybe could not be, there for me. They could not nourish me emotionally as I needed to be nourished. I needed them to bring light into my darkness, to banish the gloom that enveloped me, but they did not know how to do that. Some were so intimidated by what had happened to me that they couldn't look at me without worrying that something similar might happen to them. Some stayed away because they felt inadequate. They didn't know what to say. It bothered them to see me suffer. And some, like the friends who "comforted" Job in the Bible, offered me religious explanations that only made me feel worse. They all had their reasons for what they did, but I felt alone and rejected in the valley of the shadow. The only thing that kept me going, the only thing that let me believe in myself, was my faith in God, my faith that when I cried out, God heard me. He didn't have to do anything to solve my problem. He didn't cure my illness, He didn't find me a new job or a new mate, He didn't bring my loved one back to life. But He heard me. When I felt alone and abandoned, I prayed and I had this astonishing feeling that I was no longer alone.

The psalmist concludes, God, thank You for being there when many of my human friends weren't up to the challenge. Thank You for sustaining my faith in my own worthiness. Thank you for nourishing me with Your presence when so many others could not help me.

When human beings fail us, when friends let us down and our burdens are too much for us to bear alone, God is there to renew our strength and give us what we need to go on with our lives.

Thou Anointest My Head with Oil

Having oil poured on one's head meant something very different to the ancient Israelite than it does to us today. For a modern reader, it probably conjures up nothing more than a treatment in a beauty parlor. But in olden times, it was a great honor and an important gesture. The last person I know of to have oil poured on her head in a ritual fashion was Queen Elizabeth, when she was anointed Queen of England some fifty years ago. That ceremony, part of her investiture as queen, was a deliberate echo of the biblical ritual of anointing kings and priests, marking them as special by pouring a special ointment on their heads.

The *Random House Unabridged Dictionary* gives three definitions of the verb "to anoint," and it is fascinating to see how the meaning builds in intensity and significance from the first to the second to the third: "to apply an oily liquid; to consecrate or make sacred in a ceremony that includes the token applying of oil; to dedicate to the service of God." How did we get from smearing liquid to being dedicated to God? The ceremony of anointing with oil seems to have been an old, accepted one in biblical times. When the prophet Samuel anoints first Saul and later David to be king of Israel, there is no sense that he is inventing a new ritual, though there had never been an Israelite king before. It is assumed that everyone will understand the meaning of what he is doing. The impression given by the narratives in the Books of Samuel and Kings is that anointing does not *make* a person king. It identifies him as the one chosen by God and therefore worthy of being king. We see this most clearly in the opening chapter of the First Book of Kings. King David is old and dying, and rival priests and courtiers each have their own candidate among his sons to succeed him. One group anoints Solomon as the new king (while David is still alive, lest the others get a head start); another anoints his brother Adonijah. It takes David's deathbed intervention on Solomon's behalf to confirm his successor.

To anoint someone, then, means to say that someone is special, designated for greatness. Isn't that something we all crave, to feel that we are special, that we are recognized as unique, that there is something that we can do better than most people can? That is why some people go to extremes to be listed in *The Guinness Book of Records*, and why most of us are so gratified to have our names appear favorably in the paper. That is why a successful businessman who can afford anything he desires cherishes a twenty-five-dollar plaque given to him by his church, synagogue, or lodge as Man of the Year. And that is why many members of minority groups adopt extreme hairstyles and give their children unusual names, as a way of saying, I am not just another anonymous face in the crowd. I am somebody unique.

A passage in the Talmud reads, "The royal mint stamps out thousands of coins, each one bearing the likeness of the emperor, and each one is identical. But God fashions millions of people, each one in His image, and no two are alike. Every one of them is unique." When the psalmist writes, "Thou anointest my head with oil," he is saying, God, You have not only given me the gifts of food and safety. You have given me the gift of being special, and I accept the responsibility that comes with that gift.

What happens to the child who is never fussed over, whose birthdays are ignored, who goes to school in crowded classrooms, and whose teachers are too overworked to learn his name? Where will that child get the feeling of being one of a kind, different from anyone else who has ever lived?

In part, a child can get that sense of recognition from his or her faith, being told, Maybe your teacher can't remember your name because she has forty students to deal with, but God knows your name. And in part it is society's obligation to "anoint" that child as special in some way, before he or she grows up and is driven to do something extreme to get his or her name in the headlines. Dr. Elisabeth Kübler-Ross remembers being raised as one of identical triplets, and recalls times when she was sitting on her father's lap and realized that her father did not know which of his daughters he was holding. Growing up to be a psychiatrist, she never forgot that need to be recognized as unique.

One of the most important words in Christian and Jewish theology derives from the custom of anointing someone with oil to mark that person as special. The word is "messiah," which literally means (God's) "anointed one." (Our line from the Twenty-third Psalm uses a different verb meaning "to anoint." The sense of specialness is still there, but without the royal-messianic connotation.) Originally, the biblical concept of the messiah referred to the Israelite king, the one whose legitimacy as ruler derived not from his family or from his having seized the throne by force, but from his having been anointed by God's representative in God's name. In Isaiah's vision of the Peaceable Kingdom when the wolf will lie down with the lamb and none shall hurt or destroy (Isaiah 11), the prophet sees a world of peace and harmony coming about through the efforts of a messiah-king who will be honest and upright and concerned for the poor (the implication being that he would be unlike the corrupt, venal rulers of that time). At that point in biblical history, there was no expectation that the messiah, God's anointed one, would have any superhuman powers. Only centuries later, when the problem was not political corruption at high levels but foreign domination by Greek and Roman superpowers, did a new concept of messianic deliverance emerge. Now the messiah would have to be a superhero to defeat the superpowerful oppressor and bring about God's kingdom.

When year after year, generation after generation, the hero failed to appear, expectations split in three directions. Some people, who would go on to follow Jesus as the Christ (a Greek word meaning "the anointed one"), decided that the messianic revolution would be a revolution of the spirit rather than a military uprising, a religious rather than a political liberation. This is the significance of the exchange in Matthew 22:15–22. Someone asks Jesus if the people should withhold their tax payments, which would be an act of rebellion against Rome. Jesus answers, "Render unto Caesar what is Caesar's and unto God what is God's." That is, the messiah's task is to change hearts, not to change rulers.

A second path was chosen by mainstream Judaism after the failed revolt against Rome in the year 135 (in which the military leader of the revolt was hailed as the messiah by several leading rabbis). Most Jews decided that they and their children would live in a premessianic world, a world marked by conflict and injustice, until God in His time chose to bring down the curtain on history and usher in a brave new era.

A third interpretation, first introduced by Jewish mystics in the sixteenth century and endorsed by rational thinkers some time afterward, insisted that the problems of the world were too great for one person to solve, however gifted or powerful. Rather, every one of us had to be a "messiah in miniature," doing something, however small, to repair and redeem the world. If every one of us, like the author of the Twenty-third Psalm, feels anointed by God, if every one of us is in some way special in God's eyes, then every one of us has a responsibility to make this world a little bit more like the world God would like it to be. God is depending on us to do that.

The collapse of the great Jewish community of Spain in the fifteenth century, as Christian forces recaptured the Iberian peninsula from the Moslems and gave Jews the choice between conversion and exile, was as traumatic for the Jews of that time as the Holocaust has been for Jews of the twentieth century. Isaac Luria, the greatest Jewish theologian of his time (1534–1572), tried to make sense of the events with an elaborate theory that pictured God's world shattering into little pieces because it was too fragile and delicate to contain the intense holiness of God. As a result, humanity now lived in a broken world, a world littered with those fragments, each of them bearing the residue of God's presence. It became humanity's task to repair the world by finding those fragments, recognizing the hidden holiness of ordinary deeds and moments, and painstakingly putting the broken world back together again. Luria with his theory sought not only to explain the existence of evil in God's world, but to cure the Jewish refugees from Spain of their feelings of impotence and victimization, giving them a prominent role to play in the redemption of the world. Five hundred years after Luria's time, Jewish youth groups echo his theology when they speak of their social action projects as *tikkun olam,* "repairing the world."

Perhaps in a medieval world ruled by kings and emperors, a world where a single individual exercised absolute power over the population, it was understandable that people would think in terms of one powerful individual coming to set the world right. But in today's world, where the government presents itself as the expression of the collective will of the people, we can come to see the messianic era, the world of God's dream, ushered in not by one person doing great things but by many people doing little things. Recall the words of Mother Teresa, "Few of us can do great things but all of us can do small things with great love."

Professor Harvey Cox is a devout Christian who teaches the history of Christian thought at Harvard Divinity School. He is married to a Jewish woman, and they are raising their son as a Jew. In his fascinating book *Common Prayers,* he describes his going through the cycle of the Jewish year, experiencing the Jewish holidays through the eyes of a Christian who is a member of a committed Jewish family.

When he comes to the Seder, the ritual meal that marks

the beginning of Passover (with all of its associations with the Last Supper and the Crucifixion), Cox focuses on the moment when the family opens a door to welcome the prophet Elijah. Elijah holds a special place in Jewish folklore. For one thing, because the Bible describes him as being taken up to heaven in a fiery chariot (II Kings 2:11), the tradition arose that Elijah never died. He holds dual citizenship in heaven and on earth, and is thus in a position to commute between the two realms and alert human beings to whatever God has in store for us. Second, the last words ever spoken by a prophet in Israel (Malachi 3:23) are, "Behold I will send the prophet Elijah before the coming of that great and awesome day, and he will restore the hearts of the parents to their children and the hearts of the children to their parents." Elijah will come to set the stage for the final redemption, the advent of the messianic age.

Because Passover comes in the spring, the season when hopes are high and hearts are optimistic, the season of Israel's original redemption from Egyptian slavery, the custom arose of setting a place for Elijah at the Seder table and opening the door to greet him. It is our way of saying, Maybe this will be the year. Maybe this spring will see Elijah arrive with the good news of the imminent advent of the redemption.

During all the years of my family's celebrating Passover, I first learned and subsequently taught that interpretation of the welcoming of Elijah: maybe this will be the year. Cox, attending the Seder as a Christian and well aware of the divide between Jews and Christians over the question of whether the messiah has come or is still awaited, sees the search for Elijah from a fresh perspective. When we open the door every year and Elijah is not there, Cox suggests that we should finally realize that Elijah is not coming. And the messiah is not coming either. We have to be the messiah. We have to act together to clean up the mess we have made of the world. No one else is going to magically appear and do it for us.

When the author of the Twenty-third Psalm says to God, "You anointed my head with oil," he is saying, God, You have granted me the privilege of feeling special. You have told me that, in this vast throng of billions of people, You recognize me. But his words contain the implication that that privilege carries with it a great responsibility. That was the case for Queen Elizabeth when she was anointed with oil. In God's eyes, every one of us is royalty, not only in dignity but in our responsibility to carry out the tasks to which God has assigned us. God summons us to be alert at all times for one of the fragments of His shattered model of a perfect world, and when we find one, to pick it up, clean it off, and try to fit it into the larger picture.

There are Jewish legends about adults or children who impulsively reach out to help a beggar in rags, only to discover that the beggar is the messiah in disguise, waiting for someone to show him kindness, at which point he will reveal himself and redeem all that is broken in the world. But in today's world, perhaps it is not the beggar who is the disguised redeemer but the one who reaches out to the beggar. When we volunteer for a soup kitchen, when we staff a late-night hot line for frantic, despairing callers, when we tutor children who have difficulty learning, when we set aside our own priorities and vote for policies that will make ours a more compassionate society, we are acting as one of God's anointed. We are the messiah for somebody if not for everybody.

That is how the messianic age will arrive. That is how we will fashion a world more livable than the world we currently inhabit, a world where the wolf will lie down with the lamb and people will no longer hurt one another—not by responding to the world's brokenness as children might, by denying that we made the mess and begging or praying for someone to come and clean it up, but by responding as adults should, each of us doing our little bit to make the world whole.

We open the door and peer into the darkness. When we don't find Elijah, instead of saying, We'll have to wait for next year, let us learn to say, If Elijah is not there, let me be Elijah. God has anointed my head with oil. God expects me to do my share to bring about His kingdom. How can I not respond?

CHAPTER THIRTEEN

My Cup Runneth Over

Gratitude, I would suggest, is the fundamental religious emotion. It is where religion begins in the human heart. Gratitude, the awareness that life has given you a wonderful bounty, is an emotion of which all people should be capable, and the image of one's cup being full to overflowing is an image of gratitude.

Gratitude is more than remembering to mumble "Thank you" when someone has done you an act of kindness. It is more than an obligation, a ritual of politeness. Gratitude is a way of looking at the world that does not change the facts of your life but has the power to make your life more enjoyable.

The grateful heart understands that gratitude is a reciprocal process, giving and receiving at the same time. We *accept* a gift; we *give* thanks for it. We bless the giver with our appreciation even as the giver blesses us with his or her kindness. A Benedictine monk by the name of David Steindl-Rast has written a lovely book entitled *Gratefulness, the Heart of Prayer*. At one point, he alerts us to the way in which our language betrays us by making us think that life is mostly about taking. We take a trip, we take a vacation, we take a drive, we take an exam, we take a drink, "and finally when I am worn out by all that taking, I take a nap." But Steindl-Rast points out that we can't take those things without at the same time giving—giving our time, giving our attention, giving our thanks. "I will hardly fall asleep until I give myself to the nap and let the nap take me." We don't really *take* a vacation so much as we *give ourselves over* to the airplane, the hotel, the exotic locale we are visiting.

Gratitude is rooted in the sense that life is a gift. The essence of a gift is that it comes to you from someone else, not by your own efforts (there is something forlorn about the man who buys himself a birthday present because he has no one in his life to give him one), and as such it is a physical representation of the love and caring the giver feels toward you. A woman who receives a Mother's Day present from her five-year-old child understands that the child did not buy it with his own money, nor did he necessarily pick it out himself. But she cherishes it nonetheless as an embodiment of the child's love and wish to make her happy. What mother would sour her relationship with her child by criticizing the gift for being too small or inappropriate? Our gratitude is less for the gift than for the love of which it is a visible incarnation.

The facts of our lives—our age, our height, our gender, who our parents are, the extent of our musical or athletic abilities—are unchangeable details not of our own making. We often speak of those things as "given." To me, that is appropriate, because each of those things is a gift. God/nature/biology gave us those things, and while we might have wished for a fancier or more valuable gift (or for the freedom to exchange it), doesn't a sense of gratitude require that we accept the "givens" of our lives with thanks?

I read of a person who had formed the habit of writing "Thank you" on the lower left corner of every check he wrote. When he paid his electric bill or his phone bill, he would write "Thank you" to express his gratitude to the companies that made those services available to him at the press of a button. Even when he paid his taxes, he would write "Thank you" on the check as a way of reminding himself (he didn't think the Internal Revenue Service would notice it) that his taxes were the price he willingly paid for living in the United States with all of its benefits.

It is in that spirit that we should be grateful to God for all of His gifts to us. Would we wish to have some remarkable talent that we see others possessing? Would we prefer it if our children had remarkable talents in all areas instead of endearing qualities in just a few? To respond that way to the gift of life or the gift of a child is to be like the person who evaluates and criticizes a gift, overlooking the kindness it represents.

The remarkable thing about gratitude is that, like forgiveness, it is a favor we do ourselves more than it is something we do for the recipient of our thanks. God would have us develop the habit of gratitude for all the blessings of our lives, not because He needs our thanks but because when we acknowledge those blessings we come to feel differently about His world and live happier lives as a result. The poet W. H. Auden has written:

> . . . weather
> Is what nasty people are
> Nasty about, and the nice
> Show a common joy in observing.

Crabby people will find reasons to be crabby about the weather, whatever the day is like. It will be too hot or too cold, too rainy to go outdoors or too dry to replenish the reservoir, and if one day is perfect, it will only get worse tomorrow. They complain not because of what the day is like but because of what they are like. By contrast, grateful people are grateful for the weather whatever it may be, remembering that April showers bring May flowers.

I live in the suburbs of Boston. In the winter, when a major snowstorm is forecast, the entire region comes alive in anticipation. The weather forecast dominates the evening news. I suspect that we are responding to the prospect of extreme weather not in terms of our comfort and convenience but as a manifestation of God's power displayed in the power of nature. Snow may make driving hazardous, but snow can make the world look so beautiful that much of the time we welcome the trade-off. Nature can be destructive, giving us tornadoes and tidal waves. Nature can afflict good people and bad people indiscriminately. But nature can cause our hearts to leap with its beauty and grandeur. As unpleasant as it may be to have to drive in a blizzard or shovel the snow the next morning, there is something deeply moving about sitting safely at home with your family and looking out at the falling snow. When I was a congregational rabbi, I would periodically remind the teachers of our afternoon religious school that on the day of the first snowfall of the year, they were not to call the children back from looking out of the window to return to the lesson. A child's gasp of delighted excitement at the falling snow would be as sincere a prayer as any that would be uttered in the synagogue that day.

In the same way, the author of Psalm Twenty-nine, watching a thunderstorm over the Mediterranean, does not respond as most of us would, by worrying that the rain will flood his granary or turn the roads muddy. He sees the storm as a manifestation of the awesome power and glory of God:

The voice of the Lord is over the water,
The God of glory thunders,
The Lord, over the mighty waters.
The voice of the Lord is power;
The voice of the Lord is majesty . . .
The voice of the Lord kindles flames of fire,
The Lord convulses the wilderness of Kadesh.
   (Psalm 29:3–7)

One person sees the rain as a blessing while another sees it as a nuisance because their hearts tell their eyes how to interpret what they see. And to the grateful heart, everything is a gift from God. Psychologist Abraham Maslow has praised as a character trait of the fully mature adult "the ability to appreciate again and again, freshly and naively, the basic goods of life with awe, pleasure, wonder and even ecstasy" when others have come to take them for granted. And the essayist G. K. Chesterton puts it pithily: "Children are delighted when Santa puts toys or sweets into their stockings. Shall I not be grateful when he puts in my stockings the gift of two healthy legs?"

If gratitude is so basic and so beneficial, if it makes us happier about our lives, why is it hard for so many people to cultivate the habit of feeling grateful? I can think of two reasons. One is a sense of entitlement. If we have grown up believing that we deserve only the best, we will respond to every gift, whether from God or from friends, like the petulant child who examines a new toy and complains, "I wanted the newer model." For people who feel entitled, it is not enough to be alive and well; they resent every blemish, every limitation on their physical grace and athletic skill. It is not enough for them to have a loving partner and healthy children; they envy the glamorous romances of celebrities and the honor-roll achievements of the children next door. They are never satisfied because they measure their wealth not by what they have but by what others have that they lack.

And then there are people who have trouble feeling grateful, people who cannot bring themselves to utter the words "Thank you," because they need to feel self-sufficient. "I don't need anything from anybody. I can take care of myself." How sad not to need anybody (and how mistaken to claim that we don't). How sad not to be able to accept a gift graciously because being on the receiving end of a gift might make us feel weak and needy.

Much of the time, we have as little control over the events of our lives as we do over the weather. But as with the weather, we have a great deal of control over the way we choose to see those events and respond to them. Reading between the lines, we can infer that the author of the Twenty-third Psalm did not have a life free from pain and problems. He has had to confront enemies. He has known the feeling of finding himself in the valley of the shadow of death. He can praise and thank God for all that God has done for him, not because his life has been easy but precisely because his life has often been hard and God has seen him through the hard times. If his eyes are dim with age, he thanks God that he can still see. If his legs are stiff and his gait faltering, he thanks God that he can walk at all. If people close to him have died, he is grateful to have known their love. For the psalmist, the issue is not whether the cup is half full or half empty. Because he has learned to see everything in his life, including life itself, as a gift, his cup of blessings overflows. Because he has retained the child's ability to be surprised and delighted by the most ordinary of things, he retains many of the gifts of youth as he grows older.

Once we have learned to see our lives as the accumulation of gifts that God has given us, gifts we could not have acquired by our own efforts, once we have learned to appreciate what we have, rather than complain that we don't have more, because we could have had nothing, there are three things we can do in response.

First, we can reciprocate God's generosity by giving God our thanks and our trust: our thanks to tell Him that we appreciate His world, and our trust to tell Him that we are confident that tomorrow will bring its blessings even as yesterday did. Again, this is something we do for ourselves at least as much as for God, reminding ourselves to trust the world the way we did when we were children and to look forward to tomorrow with hope and confidence. It is of a piece with the trust that lets us thank a friend who gives us a present even before we open it, because we have faith that our friend has our best interests at heart.

Second, if we have benefited from God's generosity, it becomes our obligation to let others benefit from our generosity, or more accurately from God's generosity flowing through us to those to whom we reach out.

And the third thing we can do when we find that our cup runs over with the abundance of God's goodness is to get ourselves a bigger cup. I once gave a sermon on a Sabbath when the scriptural reading was the story about the prophet Elisha, found in II Kings 4:1–7. A poor widow comes to the prophet and laments that her husband's death left the family deeply in debt and the creditor is coming to take her sons as slaves. She has no food in the house save a small jar of oil. Elisha tells her to borrow as many jars as she can, and pour the oil into them. Magically, the oil will keep flowing until every jar is filled. She will then be able to sell the oil and settle her debts. As predicted, the oil keeps flowing until her sons tell her "there are no more vessels," at which point it stops. The point of my sermon was that our ability to enjoy God's blessings is more a function of our capacity to receive them than of any limitations on God's ability to bless us. The more blessings we are capable of finding around us, the more God will be blessing us.

Would you like to feel that your life is more blessed? Get a larger cup to receive God's blessings. Learn to see more of the "givens" of your life as gifts. Learn to respond to the sun's coming up every morning as a miracle. Steindl-Rast wrote, "Even if we knew how the whole universe worked, we [should] still be surprised that there is a universe at all." Instead of wishing that your mate could read your mind and fulfill all of your wishes, be humbly grateful that there is someone in the world to love you and put up with your quirks. Instead of wishing that you felt better physically and could lose weight more easily, marvel at your body's ability to extract nourishment from food and to heal from illness and injury. Are those not miracles?

Each night as I prepare for bed, I put drops in my eyes to fend off the threat of glaucoma that would rob me of my sight and take from me the pleasure of reading. Each morning at breakfast, I take a pill to control my blood pressure, and each evening at dinner I take another to lower my cholesterol level. But instead of lamenting the ailments that come with growing older, instead of wishing I were as young and fit as I once was, I take my medicine with a prayer of thanks that modern science has found ways to help me cope with those ailments. I think of all my ancestors who didn't live long enough to develop the complications of old age, and did not have pills to take when they did.

I read an interview with a man whose small plane had crash-landed at a California air strip. Fortunately, he was able to evacuate before the plane burst into flames. A reporter asked him what was going through his mind as the plane neared the ground. His answer: "I realized I hadn't thanked enough people in my life."

In the traditional Jewish liturgy, the first three minutes of the morning service remind the worshiper to be grateful that he is alive, that his body works, that he has food to eat and clothes to wear, that he has things to do today that will demonstrate his humanity, and that he has friends to share the day with. Our ability to receive God's blessings with thanksgiving will never outstrip God's ability to bless us. For those who have cultivated the habit of gratitude, no matter how large a bowl we set out to receive God's blessings, it will always overflow.

CHAPTER FOURTEEN

Surely Goodness and Mercy Shall Follow Me All the Days of My Life

At first glance, this verse may simply be a continuation of the previous one: Once I have learned to look at the world with eyes of gratitude, I see all the wonderful things that God does for me, and I am confident that God will continue to do them. But notice the verb: "goodness and mercy shall *follow* me. . . ." The force of the original Hebrew is even stronger: "goodness and mercy shall *pursue* me. . . ." That is, they will not only accompany me and bless my life. They will run after me and find me wherever I am.

It calls to mind the story of the rabbi who stops a prominent member of his congregation in the street and says to him, "Whenever I see you, you're always in a hurry. You're always rushing somewhere. Tell me, what are you running after all the time?" The man answers, "I'm running after success, I'm running after prosperity, I'm running to make a good living." The rabbi responds, "That's a good answer, if you assume that all of those rewards are out there ahead of you, trying to elude you, and you have to run hard to catch up to them. But what if the rewards are behind you, looking for you, but they can never find you because you're running away from them? What if God has all sorts of wonderful gifts He wants to give you, but you're never home when He comes looking for you so He can't deliver them?"

Recall Einstein's question: Is the universe a friendly place? Is it full of wonderful things waiting for us to claim them and enjoy them? Or do we have to fight and struggle for everything we need to make our lives feel fulfilled? The answer, I believe, is: both. There are some blessings that will be ours only if we work hard to earn them. The gifted athlete who relies on talent and does not work at his sport is setting himself up for disappointment. The young couple who believe that love and physical attraction will be enough to guarantee their living happily ever after will soon encounter frustration. It takes a lot of hard work to build a successful marriage. It takes a lot of hard work to build a successful career, no matter how easy it may look to an outsider. Just being a nice person who *deserves* to be happy isn't enough.

But then there are other blessings that will be ours only if we stop chasing after them and let them come to us, like the butterfly that eludes our grasp when we try to catch it but comes to perch on our shoulder when we stop chasing it and sit still. We are made uncomfortable by the politician who is too transparently ambitious, no sooner elected to one office than he begins to scheme to run for a higher one. The young man or woman who is too desperate to form a serious relationship will often put a potential partner off with his or her impatience and frantic intensity. I think of the young woman in my community who went to every singles event she knew of, read the personal ads, signed up with introduction agencies, all to no avail. Finally, out of a deep sense of frustration, she gave up her full-time husband-hunting and decided to spend a year doing things she enjoyed rather than the things recommended in the magazines for single women. She volunteered; she took classes. It didn't take long for her more relaxed persona to make her seem more attractive to the eligible men she met.

Look again at the biblical verse. It doesn't say, surely fame and fortune will come to me without my having to work for them. I'll buy a lottery ticket and rely on God to make me rich. It doesn't say, surely I will instinctively know how to be a good mate, a good parent, without giving it a lot of thought. It says, If I stop pursuing happiness so strenuously and just relax, *goodness and mercy* will find their way into my life. Goodness has been defined as feeling good about life, feeling good about oneself: I'm happy being me. There are things I may not have, but I'm fine without them. Mercy has been defined as the discovery of forgiveness in the world, the experience of being given things we may not have earned and may not be sure we deserve.

To say that the blessing of contentment will follow you is an important theological statement, perhaps one of the most important and most liberating truths we can be told about the world. It says: You may have to work hard to earn your living. You may have to work hard to be an effective wife, husband, or parent. You may have to work hard to care for aging parents or ill relatives. But you don't have to work hard in order to feel good about yourself. All you have to do is stop striving, relax, and say to yourself, I feel good about who I am. There may be people who have been trying to break a bad habit for years. I suspect that they might be more successful if they told themselves, "I feel good about who I am," rather than constantly telling themselves, "What's the matter with me? Why do I have so little self-control?"

I remember sitting with a teenage girl in my congregation who had just been diagnosed with a chronic illness that would severely limit her ability to do things that teenagers do—swimming, dancing, skiing. I said to her, "Don't let this illness define who you are. Ninety-eight percent of you is just fine; there's just one little part of you that doesn't work right. Focus on the ninety-eight percent. You're still bright, attractive, caring, funny. Those are things your condition can't take away from you unless you let it. The choice is yours."

We can't choose to be healthy, to be attractive, to be talented. But we can choose to like ourselves as we are, whether that includes those blessings or not. We don't have to chase after contentment the way we have to chase after fame and fortune. We just have to hold still and let it find us, wherever we are in our lives.

The claim of the psalmist that we don't have to achieve mercy, that it too will find us, is an equally important lesson for us to grasp. Whole books have been written about the meaning of the Hebrew word "*hesed,*" here translated as "mercy," more commonly rendered "lovingkindness." I like to think of *hesed* as "unearned love." In interpersonal terms, *hesed* asks us (it does not demand; love cannot be commanded) to go beyond the letter of the law in order to fashion a more human world. It asks us to do things for others that we don't have to do and that the other party might not deserve, but we should do them anyway.

The Talmud tells the story of a wealthy vineyard owner who learns that one of his workers has accidentally spilled a cask of expensive wine. The owner takes the worker to court, suing him for the value of the wine. The court tells him, "Clearly the law is on your side and you are entitled to damages. But the worker is a poor man. Not only has he no money to pay you; he depends on his daily wage to feed his family. You are not only a wealthy man, you are widely known to be a pious man. The court cannot compel you but it would urge you to act on the basis of *hesed,* not only to drop the charges but to pay your worker his daily wage. It may diminish your wealth slightly but it will enrich you in other ways. Think of it as a small step toward making the world a nicer place, and may God forgive you for your mistakes as you forgive your hired man." The Talmud goes on to say that the man complied.

Unearned love—is there really any other kind? Can we persuade someone that they ought to love us? Has a parent ever won an argument with a child by itemizing "after all we've done for you"? Is a marriage ever strengthened by one partner keeping a list of all the things he or she has gone out of his or her way to do for the other without being reciprocated? Love is never a matter of owing someone for favors done. Love is a way of saying, I know all of your good qualities and all of your exasperating qualities, and because I like who I am when I am with you and I like who we are when we're together, I buy the package.

Is the psalmist's confident prayer that *hesed* will follow him all the days of his life an expression of hope that people will treat him mercifully, loving him enough to forgive him when he needs forgiveness? Or is it a prayer that *he* will be blessed with the capacity to be merciful, to be forgiving, all the days of his life? Probably both. The prophet Hosea, after picturing Israel as an unfaithful wife in its relationship to God, cites God as promising, "I will betroth you unto Me with righteousness and justice, with steadfast love [*hesed*] and kindness" (Hosea 2:19). Many commentators understand the verse as God's promising not only to forgive Israel out of His love for them, but also to bless Israel with the capacity to be righteous and steadfastly loving, so that the relationship will prosper in the future. I have often used that verse when speaking to a bride and groom at their wedding, praying that God's wedding present to them be the ability to love and forgive each other.

When the psalmist speaks of "goodness and mercy following him *all the days of [his] life,*" I understand that as a vision of a world where goodness and mercy will characterize every stage of the lifespan, where adolescents will be merciful to one another instead of treating one another cruelly out of their own insecurity, a world where husbands and wives will bless each other with unearned love instead of "keeping score," a world where the elderly will find contentment in the last chapters of their lives because people will treat them with respect and honor, "forgiving" them for the limitations that old age might impose on them. I hear it as a prayer that as he grows older, he will never become the cranky old man who resents younger people for their liveliness, their sexual energy, the possibilities still open to them in their lives, because he will have retained the gift of contentment and mercy all of his days.

We cannot, nor do we need to, persuade God that

we deserve His *hesed,* His unearned love. But when the psalmist writes "*Surely* goodness and mercy shall follow me . . . ," he is expressing confidence, born of all his experiences with God, that he will be blessed with God's love, not because of who he is but because of who God is.

CHAPTER FIFTEEN

And I Shall Dwell in the House of the Lord Forever

We can read the Twenty-third Psalm as a drama in three acts. Act one is serene, pastoral. The psalmist feels safe and secure, and he thanks God, his faithful shepherd, for providing him with that security. Act two turns dark and stormy. The psalmist's life is interrupted by trauma, tragedy, and bereavement. Instead of dwelling in green pastures by still waters, he finds himself alone in a dark valley. Then he learns that he is not really alone. He comes to see God not only as the source of the good things in his life, but as the source of comfort and consolation in hard times. He comes to understand that only because God was with him was he able to find his way out of the darkness. He learns, as all of us who have gone through hard times learn, that the sunshine we step into when we have found our way through the valley of the shadow is infinitely sweeter than the sunshine we had basked in during our carefree, cloudless days. In act three, he realizes that his understanding of God, his relationship to God, has matured as well. God is no longer just the one who follows him through his travails. God now offers him something more permanent, an invitation to dwell in His house.

What does it mean to dwell in the house of the Lord? "Home" is such an evocative word. It speaks of love, of an enduring relationship. Robert Frost defines it as "something you somehow don't have to deserve." It is the ultimate expression of the promise, "I will be with you." Home symbolizes safety, security, a refuge from the dangers of the world outside. God's house is also a sanctuary in the sense of a holy place (*sanctus* means holy).

But there is also a sense in which it is uncomfortable, even intimidating to live our days conscious of the fact that we are living them in God's presence. A Hassidic tale tells of the rabbi who hired a horse and carriage to take him to a neighboring village. The carriage was making its way along a road with fruit trees and orchards on either side. At one point, the coachman stopped by the side of the road and told his passenger, "I'm going to climb over the fence and steal some of that fruit. You sit here and keep an eye out for anyone coming. Let me know if anyone sees me." He had just crossed the fence when the rabbi called out, "Someone's watching!" The driver jumped back into his wagon, drove a bit farther, stopped, and said, "I'm going to try again. Make sure I'm not being seen." Once again, as soon as he crossed the fence, the rabbi called out, "Someone's watching!" The driver was puzzled. He said, "I don't understand it. The road is empty; the area is deserted. I don't see another human being for miles. But every time I try to grab some fruit, you tell me someone's watching. What's going on?" The rabbi pointed heavenward and said simply, "Someone is watching."

For the author of the Twenty-third Psalm, dwelling in God's house, having the sense that every moment of his day is being lived under God's watchful eye, is the most reassuring, most comforting thought he can have. For the rabbi's coachman, it is a major inconvenience, keeping him from doing things he would like to do. What might it mean to us? The answer may depend on where we are in our lives.

For a young child, there are few things more important and reassuring than the knowledge that his parent is there watching out for him, and few things more unsettling than the fear that the parent might not be there. That is likely why very young children play peek-a-boo; its message: Mommy may go away out of sight, but she comes back a moment later. That may be why young children in a playground "push the envelope," going to the brink of doing something dangerous or forbidden, not in the hope of getting away with it but in an effort to elicit the reassuring cry of "Stop that, I'm watching you." And maybe there is a part of us that never quite outgrows that childhood need.

But a few years later, that young child grows into a sulky, withdrawn teenager. "Momma, come see what I can do" is replaced by "Stay out of my room" and "Will you just get off my back and let me live my life?" What has happened? One of the defining characteristics of adolescence is self-consciousness, the feeling that people are looking at you and judging you. For the first time in their lives, adolescents are making ethical decisions, making choices about their values and their behavior without parental guidance and authority. They are making choices about dress, relationships, and money, and because they can never be sure they are doing it right, they are manifestly uncomfortable, hypersensitive to being judged. If you have a fourteen-year-old daughter at home (or if you can remember being a fourteen-year-old girl), how much time does she spend on the phone with her friends every evening deciding what to wear to school the next day? It is important for her to know that she won't stand out as the only one wearing the "wrong" clothes.

Go back and reread chapter three of Genesis, the puzzling story of Adam and Eve in the Garden of Eden. Note that before Adam and Eve eat the forbidden fruit, they are described as "naked but feeling no shame" (Genesis 2:25). But the very first thing that happens after they eat of the Tree of the Knowledge of Good and Evil is that they realize they are naked, feel embarrassed by it, and try to hide from God's sight. Why are they ashamed when there is literally no one else in the world to see them? My understanding of the story is that acquiring a knowledge of good and evil marks their transition from childhood to adolescence. Isn't that the difference between a child and a teenager, that a child can only be obedient or disobedient to parents and teachers, but a teenager has to make his or her own moral decisions about right and wrong a thousand times a day? I see Adam and Eve after they eat the forbidden fruit as adolescents, brand-new to the world of knowing right and wrong, new to the challenge of making moral choices, insecure about their body image, uncomfortable at the prospect of being judged, risking being told that they had done wrong and would be punished.

According to some classical Christian and Jewish interpretations of the Garden of Eden story, Adam and Eve were capable of sexual activity and reproduction even before they ate the forbidden fruit. Remember, they were commanded to be fruitful and multiply. But after they ate the fruit and acquired a knowledge of good and evil, their attitude toward sexuality changed. It was no longer a simple matter of being guided by nature and instinct, as it is for other animals. It now took on a frantic dimension, a quest for intimacy and closeness, a reprieve from loneliness, a reassurance of being desired. (Sounds very adolescent to me.)

For Adam and Eve, for the rabbi's coachman, for the typical adolescent, living in the presence of God is intimidating, a source of potential shame and imminent condemnation. When Job's friends try to comfort him after a series of disasters have made his life miserable, they speak to him in the accents of childhood: Don't despair, our heavenly Father is watching over us constantly. And Job responds like an adolescent: You're right, God is always watching over us—to catch us in a mistake and have a reason to punish us (Job 7:20).

As we grow older, we carry with us fragments of both views, the child's sense of reassurance that his parents are there for him and the adolescent's need for a life free of watchful eyes and judgmental authorities. Ultimately we come up with an outlook that reconciles the two. We come to realize that God invites us into His house, into His presence, not simply to protect us and not only to judge us, but to establish a relationship with us, and the basis of that relationship is God's expectation of moral behavior. God says to us, as one might say to a child who is no longer a child, If you are going to live in My house, I expect certain things of you. God says this not in order to restrict us or to punish us when He catches us in a mistake, but to show that He takes us seriously and to invest our lives with significance by telling us that He cares how we live.

In the view of Rabbi Joseph Soloveitchik, one of the great souls of the American Jewish community, God gave Israel the Law at Mount Sinai because He sensed the existential loneliness of the average human being in what can often be a lonely world. God who created Eve as Adam's mate because "it is not good for man to be alone" sought to cure an even deeper feeling of loneliness by reaching down to enter into people's lives, freeing the Israelites from Egypt and forming a covenant with them. For Soloveitchik, as paraphrased by one of his disciples, there comes a point in a person's life when he or she realizes that one's "work does not suffice to define [one's] personality. Human dignity is now seen in the quest for purpose, meaning and relationship." With the sound of God's voice addressing man by name (that is, when we feel personally commanded to do something we might otherwise not be inclined to do—being generous, forgiving, in control of our emotions), "God, whom Man has searched for along the endless trails of the universe, is suddenly discovered as standing beside him."

God, who is pure righteousness, seeks to establish a relationship with human beings by summoning us to do righteous deeds. In that way, God connects with our soul, our conscience, the little bit of Himself that He breathed into us, that inner voice that should have told the coachman that it was wrong to steal his neighbor's fruit even if he didn't have a rabbi as his passenger. God tried to do that with Adam, giving him one command. But Adam, too much the adolescent, was unprepared for a mature relationship with God. When God called Noah, Abraham, or Moses to do things that were challenging but right, promising only that He would be with them, promising to guide Abraham to his unknown destination, telling Moses "I will be with you" (Exodus 3:11–12) when he asked, "Who am I that I should go to Pharaoh?," that was more than an assignment. It was an invitation to a relationship. For the person who asks, "Why should I be good? Why should I respect my neighbor's property? Where is my reward for being honest?," the Twenty-third Psalm gives us the answer. The reward is "I shall dwell in the House of the Lord forever." The reward is that you will be redeemed from the existential loneliness of wandering aimlessly through life, without meaning or purpose. You will have God as your friend and neighbor.

And what will be the punishment for the person who chooses to live a selfish, deceitful, exploitative life? I don't need to picture him tormented in Hell and cast into fire and brimstone. It is punishment enough that he will live out his days alone, perhaps feared, perhaps envied, but ultimately alone where it matters most, while those around him live out their days in the presence of God.

Can you remember a time when you went out of your way to help a neighbor in need, and how good that felt? Can you remember a time when you reluctantly gave money to a good cause because you could not say no to the person who asked you, and later you realized what a bargain you had gotten? The feeling of satisfaction you got from helping those in need was worth more to you than the money. That is what it means to live in the House of the Lord, to have a relationship with God based not on our need and not on His might but on the capacity for righteous living that God has planted in each of us.

There is a part of us that wants to live in the presence of God, not only for the comfort but for the challenge. There is a part of us that wants to be summoned, that welcomes the demands of morality and righteousness. When God summons us to act justly and righteously, it is His way of telling us that He takes us seriously enough to care about how we live. When He tells our neighbors not to harm us, not to harm our marriage, our property, our reputation, He is giving us the message that He cares about our well-being. When He speaks to us through the voice of our conscience and through the words and deeds of inspiring teachers and leaders, He is assuring us that we are not alone in a dangerous and distracting world. When we come to understand that, we learn to see our lives differently. We learn to see our pain and our problems differently. We learn to see the world differently.

The author of the Twenty-third Psalm, who has been meditating on all the good things that God does for him, has saved the best for last. God, who has provided him with a peaceful, livable world, who has stilled the raging waters around him and within him, who has led him through the valley of the shadow, has also given him this ultimate gift: He has invited him into His home, into His presence, that he might live all of his days in the presence of God. God has said to him in his bereavement, as he languished in the valley of the shadow, You have lost someone you love, but you have found Me. You have discovered what I am really about, not the God of fairy tales and contrived happy endings, but the God who said to Abraham, to Joseph, to Moses, to the saints and strivers in every generation, "Fear not for I will be with you." You have found Me, and I will not abandon you. Like the shepherd who watches his flock by day and at night, I will be with you in sunshine and in shadow, in happy times and in tragic times. My house is your home.

The psalmist, I am sure, repaid God with prayers of gratitude and with acts of righteousness. But in addition, he repaid God for all of His kindnesses by writing a psalm, so that future generations would come to know what he had come to know about God. And this is what he has to tell us:

When we are frightened because the world is a scary place, God is with us. If He cannot always protect us from harm or from our own mistakes, He can ease our fears and our pain by being with us.

When we are exhausted because the world asks so much of us, God gives us times and places of refuge from the claims of the world, to calm and restore our souls. God renews our strength so that we can "mount up with wings as eagles" and continue tirelessly to do what is right.

When we are terrified at the prospect of losing control over our emotions and doing ourselves serious harm, God is with us to help us do things with Him at our side that we were not sure we could do alone.

When illness, bereavement, and the losses that come

with age cast a shadow over our lives, God is there to fill the empty space, to remind us that shadows are cast only because the sun is shining somewhere, to take us by the hand and lead us through the valley of the shadow and into the sunlight.

When events in our world bring us dismay and we fear that evil is prospering, God reminds us that evil acts invariably carry the seeds of their own destruction.

When people disappoint us, when they cannot give us what we need, whether because our needs are too great or because their emotional resources are too meager, God is our reliable friend, an inexhaustible source of love and strength.

And when we find ourselves wandering aimlessly through the world, wondering why we are here and what our lives will have meant when they are over, God blesses us with a sense of purpose, a challenge, a list of moral obligations and opportunities, every one of which will give us the sense of living our days in His presence.

There is pain in the world. If we are to be truly alive, we cannot hide from it. But we can survive it, and God's caring presence lessens the pain.

There is death in the world, robbing us of the ones we love and one day robbing them of our presence. But God who is immortal assures us that death may take a person out of our future but cannot remove him from our past, that all the things we loved a person for have entered so deeply into our souls that they remain part of us. The

Lord gives, but the Lord does not take away, and their presence is every bit as real as their absence.

There is fear in the world. There is vulnerability and uncertainty. God cannot tell us that nothing bad will ever happen to us. But God can tell us that we need not be afraid of the future, no matter what it holds. He cannot protect you from evil without taking away from other people the human power of choosing between good and bad. He cannot protect you from illness or bad luck. He cannot spare you from death and let you and those around you live forever. But He can give you the resources to transcend and overcome those fears, so that bad luck never causes you to lose faith in yourself, so that bad people never cause you to lose faith in humanity, so that the inevitability of death never causes you to give up on the holiness of life.

There will be dark days, days of loss and days of failure, but they will not last forever. The light will always return to chase away the darkness, the sun will always come out again after the rain, and the human spirit will always rise above failure. Fear will assault us, but we will not be afraid, "for Thou art with me."

A NOTE ABOUT THE AUTHOR

Harold S. Kushner, a native of Brooklyn, is Rabbi Laureate of Temple Israel in Natick, Massachusetts. He is the author of eight previous books, including *When Bad Things Happen to Good People,* chosen by the members of the Book-of-the-Month Club as one of the ten most influential books in their lives. He has been honored by the Christophers as one of fifty people who have made the world a better place, and by Religion in American Life as their clergyman of the year in 1999. He and his wife live in Natick.

A NOTE ON THE TYPE

The text of this book was set in Sabon, a typeface designed by Jan Tschichold (1902–1974), the well-known German typographer. Based loosely on the original designs by Claude Garamond (c. 1480–1561), Sabon is unique in that it was explicitly designed for hot-metal composition on both the Monotype and Linotype machines as well as for filmsetting. Designed in 1966 in Frankfurt, Sabon was named for the famous Lyons punch cutter Jacques Sabon, who is thought to have brought some of Garamond's matrices to Frankfurt.

Composed by Creative Graphics,
Allentown, Pennsylvania

Printed and bound by R. R. Donnelley & Sons,
Crawfordsville, Indiana

Designed by M. Kristen Bearse